ROUTLEDGE LIBRARY EDITIONS:
POLITICAL SCIENCE

LAW, SOCIALISM
AND DEMOCRACY

GW00601330

LAW, SOCIALISM AND DEMOCRACY

By

PAUL Q. HIRST

Volume 9

Routledge
Taylor & Francis Group

LONDON AND NEW YORK

First published 1986

This edition first published in 2010
by Routledge
2 Park Square, Milton Park, Abingdon, Oxon, OX14 4RN

Simultaneously published in the USA and Canada
by Routledge
711 Third Avenue, New York, NY 10017

First issued in paperback 2012
Routledge is an imprint of the Taylor & Francis Group, an informa business

British Library Cataloguing in Publication Data
A catalogue record for this book is available from the British Library

ISBN 13: 978-0-415-49111-2 (Set)

Publisher's Note
The publisher has gone to great lengths to ensure the quality of
this reprint but points out that some imperfections in the original
copies may be apparent.

Disclaimer
The publisher has made every effort to trace copyright holders and
would welcome correspondence from those they have been unable
to trace.

ISBN13: 978-0-415-64964-3 (PBK)

ISBN13: 978-0-415-55540-1 (HBK)

LAW, SOCIALISM AND DEMOCRACY

Paul Q. Hirst

Professor of Social Theory, Birkbeck College,
University of London

London
ALLEN & UNWIN
Boston   Sydney

**Allen & Unwin (Publishers) Ltd,
40 Museum Street, London WC1A 1LU, UK**

Allen & Unwin (Publishers) Ltd,
Park Lane, Hemel Hempstead, Herts HP2 4TE, UK

Allen & Unwin, Inc.,
8 Winchester Place, Winchester, Mass. 01890, USA

Allen & Unwin (Australia) Ltd,
8 Napier Street, North Sydney, NSW 2060, Australia

First published in 1986

British Library Cataloguing in Publication Data

Hirst, Paul Q.
    Law, socialism and democracy.
1. Socialism   2. Democracy
I. Title
335.5   HX73
ISBN 0–04–301253–1
ISBN 0–04–301254–X Pbk

Library of Congress Cataloging-in-Publication Data

Hirst, Paul Q.
    Law, socialism, and democracy.
Bibliography: p.
Includes index.
1. Democracy.   2. Constitutional law.   3. Socialism.
I. Title.
JC421.H57   1986   320′.01′1   86–1111
ISBN 0–04–301253–1 (alk. paper)
ISBN 0–04–301254–X (pbk.: alk. paper)

Set in 10 on 12 point Bembo by Nene Phototypesetters, Northampton
and printed in Great Britain by Billing and Sons Ltd, London and Worcester

Contents

Acknowledgements

The following chapters were originally published as follows:

Chapter 2 in *Radical Issues in Criminology*, P. Carlen and M. Collison (eds), Oxford: Martin Robertson, 1980;
Chapter 3 in *Economy and Society*, Vol. 14, No. 1, February 1985;
Chapter 4 in the *International Journal of the Sociology of Law*, No. 13, 1985;
Chapter 7 in *Law in Context* (Melbourne), No. 2, 1984.

The author wishes to thank the editors and publishers for their kind permission to republish these articles here. Chapters 5 and 6 were given as papers to the Socialist Philosophy Group, organized by the Fabian Society. Chapter 5 was published as an Occasional Paper by the Group.

I am grateful to Mark Cousins, Stephan Feuchtwang and Jonathan Zeitlin for their help and advice. Barry Hindess' assistance and ideas are an essential part of this book and it should be read in conjunction with his *Parliamentary Democracy and Socialist Politics*.

1   *Introduction*

This book is concerned with the political institutions and the legal framework necessary for a democratic socialism. I have pursued this theme over a number of years in a critical dialogue with Marxism and with liberal political theory. It may appear to be quixotic to pursue it as I do in the mid-1980s when there are so many immediate evils to be confronted – poverty and unemployment, racial oppression and its grim reflection of riot and murder. I see my critics very clearly and they fall into two different categories. I owe both of them an answer and they in turn need to think again and carefully about their own questions.

To the renascent Labour centre all such theorizing is a diversion from the essential task of winning the next election. *Theorizing* democratic socialism rather than sloganizing it, pursuing the argument into the radical political changes needed for a democratic socialist society, is not only diversionary but dangerous. It offers the Conservative enemy the dangerous radicalism it desperately needs in order to denounce Labour. The boat is always in danger of being rocked and there are always urgent and attainable reforms to be pursued after the next electoral victory. This is not to deny or to belittle the urgency of working for electoral victory today; far from it. It is simply to say that one must have a clear view – not a 'vision' – of the attainable radical changes – not a utopia – that lie beyond the tunnel vision of the 'next' election. Without the political preparation for radical change, the series of 'next' elections is infinite. Part of that preparation is political theorizing to convert socialism into a specific and practical political doctrine – changing it from an anti–capitalist economic theory and a set of values and political sentiments into an account of a new and superior constitution, of political institutions that permit both democratic accountability and efficient government.

To some of the radical Left, increasingly fragmented and

despairing, the idea of building a democratic socialism by the existing democratic means is absurd. They see Britain through an apocalyptic lens: a society crumbling at its very foundations, and a polity so indifferent to suffering that it will eventually be burst asunder by mass protest and resistance. The task is to facilitate that resistance, to aid workers, blacks, women, the peace movements, etc., in their struggles against authority. But the apocalypse never comes; the poor never do inherit the earth, or, less meek and mildly, seize it gun-in-hand. Britain is a land not merely of poverty, un-employment and squalor, but also of comfort and modest plenty for masses of ordinary working people. It is not a citadel of the few bloated rich to be assaulted by the mass of starveling poor. It remains possible, if not likely, to persuade a majority of ordinary people, manual and non-manual workers, that we can tackle the evils of poverty, unemployment and squalor and that we can do so without an authoritarian and regimented society, indeed, that in doing so we can greatly increase the level of accountability and participation.

A RADICAL REVISION OF M-L POLITICAL THEORY & POLITICS ARE PROPOSED

Since 1848 it has been clear that the poor cannot change things by revolutionary mass struggle; they will be shot to pieces or otherwise contained by the organized forces of repression. Only if the government, army and police are divided and disorganized, if political and social forces are violently polarized in the higher social strata, can revolutionary political change come about. This is what the Marxist–Leninist tradition, which digested thoroughly the lessons of 1848 and 1870–71, called the 'national crisis'. Leninism continued insurrectionary thinking as a viable general political response to the Western world only because it also believed in a general evolution of capitalism that would bring these crises about. If no such general tendency exists then such national crises are adventitious and conjunctural and, therefore, no general political response is possible. In other words, there is no alternative to political struggle with the forces and arenas at hand, which in Western Europe means political parties and electoral competition.

Socialism has known this for a hundred years. It has built political parties and competed in elections, it has assisted in the building of trades unions and the organization of labour, and it has participated in central and local governments to change and reform social conditions. Yet all this time it has been locked into structures of thought and politics (revolution versus reform, utopia versus pragmatism) that deny it the full benefits of its knowledge. It is hard to deny that the construction of a democratic socialism by the existing democratic means is difficult, but both of these opposed positions have perceived it to be impossible. The revolutionaries perceive a world where political means are tainted: representative democracy, formal law and government action are despised as incapable of radical improvement. They therefore cling to the apocalypse and, after it, to a society entirely different from the present one – a society without the state and a democratic life without organized political pluralism. The reformists, in contrast, cleave to existing institutions and the maximum immediate benefits that can be milked from them. Quite rightly, they prefer the lesser evil. But they, too, perceive existing political institutions and forms of social organization as incapable of *radical* improvement.

Reformist socialists have played a major role in the construction of big government and the institutions of mass welfare. They have been not merely conservative but innovative in using political democracy to change the world. They have built up the activities of state whilst leaving the institutions of democracy largely untouched and unreformed. In consequence, they have helped to reduce the effectiveness of democracy and with it radical action for reform, and thus have exacerbated the reformist dilemma. Radical change now depends on a revitalization of democracy and, therefore, on the reform of political institutions. The agencies of big government need to be made more accountable and responsive to the needs of those they administer. Socialists must therefore now enter the dangerous ground of proposing radical reforms in *political* institutions – 'tampering with the constitution' as the Conservatives and all other reactionaries will bray.

We can only do this if we believe in and are seen to believe in the basic values of the system we wish to change; that is, in representative democracy, in social pluralism and in legally codified and defended civil rights of opposition and political action. Revolutionaries have despised these things and reformists taken them for granted as part of the *status quo*. But they are now a *threatened* part of the *status quo*. A radical and democratic socialism cannot embrace big government as a neutral and efficient means to its ends nor can it subordinate politics to economic theory. The results of doing so are self-evidently the biggest threats to popular support for socialist politics. Socialism is always challenged in the West by its caricature in the Eastern bloc.

We must start in this process of being seen to be committed to democratic values by abandoning the view of socialism as an economic system entirely distinct in its nature from capitalism, and whose primary values are the efficiency of centrally planned production and the egalitarian fairness of bureaucratically administered non-commodity distribution. This is what we are too often saddled with, this side of the non-political utopia in which scarcity has been abolished. The utopian fairy stories are seldom peddled now for fear of open derision, but we have only just begun to recognize that the central features of the 'socialism' that remains are a liability. People do not need a von Mises to tell them that what is called 'central planning' is not very efficient or a von Hayek to tell them that existing forms of non-commodity distribution do not exhibit much egalitarian fairness either. We need not in consequence swallow that alternative phantom of economic sorcery, the 'market'. Central planning versus markets is as negative and baleful an opposition as revolution versus reform. In fact, the socialist movement has shown a great diversity in its economic thinking and fortunately it continues to do so today. A democratic socialist society must necessarily admit of diverse forms of economic organization and calculation. That is necessary, on the one hand, to avoid the *economic* pitfalls of economic dogmatism (that is, to allow for the benefits of learning and evolution, competition and adaptation on the part of the diverse economic agents) and, on the other hand, to serve as one of the causes for genuine social differences and alternatives, to give people choices in ways of living.

Such an approach is more consistent with radical, but nevertheless, evolutionary change, a development from existing social relations rather than a complete break that inaugurates an entirely new system governed by a distinct principle. It is time we did away with the religious elements in Hegel and the Hegelian elements in Marx. Such an approach is also consistent with developing and extending parliamentary democracy, which no longer appears as a merely 'bourgeois' creation to be replaced by an entirely new 'popular' democracy in which the masses are full participants. Such a popular democracy exists nowhere in the advanced world, nor could it. The technical needs of specialist administration and the social differentiation produced by a complex division of labour obliterate the competence and fragment the coherence of the 'masses'. Modern democracy, like modern industry, cannot continue to develop on the basis of the simplistic products of opposed sorceries. If the economic wizards fight with the simplistic formulaic spells of market versus plan, the political wizards continue to contrast parliamentary and popular democracy as opposed principles and systems of political organization sufficient in themselves. Modern democratic polities must be complex combinations of different political mechanisms.

The essays in this book explore the possibilities of democratic socialist political organization and consider such combinations of political mechanisms. They are investigatory rather than systematic. Chapters 2–5 discuss explicitly the political and legal framework of a democratic socialism. Chapter 6 considers industrial democracy in the context of the need to modernize British manufacturing industry. Chapter 7 may appear an anomaly since it concerns forms of punishment and their validity, although Chapter 3 also touches on this question. It is included both because it raises general questions about the nature of legal regulation and the character of legal sanctions and because it offers a caution against relying on force and punishment as means to attain specific ends. Certain socialists are all too willing in their imaginations to fill the prisons and keep the firing squads busy in order to eliminate reactionaries and 'class enemies'. The conclusion of Chapter 7 is that any civilized polity that continued and extended liberal and democratic objectives would seek to punish as little as possible and in particular to explore how few people we could send to prison. At a time when rabid hysteria about 'law and order' leads to filling prisons beyond capacity and to building new prisons to 'house' people who have never lived in a proper home, this seemed an essential rather than a peripheral part of a book on law and democratic socialism.

The essays collected here were written at different times and mark my evolution away from a populist variant of Marxism. In consequence some of the arguments vary in their terms and emphases. When I began I was defensive about representative democracy and social pluralism. But all the ambiguity does not stem from me alone – the word and the concept 'pluralism' connote a complex of interrelated meanings. In distinguishing these different nuances I may offer clarification to the reader and some account of the continuing themes running across these essays. 'Pluralism' is used in four distinct senses:

(1)   As the name for a specific current in Western political theory. From de Tocqueville to Dahl it has been argued that a plurality of competing political forces within a stable institutionalized framework is a precondition for individual liberty and further that, as a consequence of that competition, these forces must have some reasonable chance of nominating key decision-making personnel or of influencing decisions. At no point in these essays will one find a simple-minded attack on 'bourgeois pluralism', still regrettably so much a part of social scientific radicalism. At the same time, particularly in Chapter 2, 'pluralism' is approached warily and critically, for it is quite clear that most of the authors in this tradition are conservatives and that they would oppose root and branch any attempt to enable the Left and radical forces to profit by such political competition.

(2)   As a specific reference to one of the central propositions in that current of theory. It is argued that the existence of independent and organized social groups is the basis for effective political competition and a guarantee that the temporary victors in this competition do not carry all before them and put an end to the process whereby they have come to power. Therefore, a precondition for political liberty is a society that has sources of difference outside of politics and that has organized 'secondary associations' stemming from these differences and independent of state direction. This proposition, expressed in this general form, seems to me incontestable. However, it has been contested, for two main reasons, both of which concern specific extensions of the proposition and are not intrinsic to it.

The first is that de Tocqueville's argument about secondary associations not subordinate to state control has been extended into the dubious theory of 'totalitarianism'. This concept denotes a society in which all spheres of life are controlled and directed by a dominant mass party at the service of dictatorial leaders who have undisputed control of state power. Law is at the convenience of the rulers and they use state and party to mobilize the masses in order to realize ideological objectives. All aspects of life are, therefore, subject to politically imposed norms and there is no legal defence of a private sphere against the imposition of these norms. No variant of this concept can generate a credible description of an actual political system. The reason is that there cannot be a state in which all genuine social differences and interests are eliminated and in which political forces do not compete to influence decisions. This may have been the *aim* of certain 'totalitarian' political forces, such as the Nazi Party, but it is the actuality of no political system. In so-called 'totalitarian' societies certain political forces and interests are suppressed and denied influence, but competing elites exist and contend for power – not through elections but through less open, if very real, competition of bureaucratic infighting. Such elite competition and the restricted active participation of the masses mirror in caricature forms some of the more minimalist democratic elitist accounts of democracy.

In fact, 'totalitarian' societies, far from being highly centralized and organized, are often much less so than are representative democratic states. In such societies competing bureaucracies over-lap in their competencies and seek to extend their power by building up networks of clients. No better example of such unregulated bureaucratic competition and the administrative and political chaos consequent upon it can be found than the Nazi state. Liberal political theory and the concept of totalitarianism none the less identify pluralism and open political competition with representative demo-cracy. This identification involves a theoretical *non sequitur* (even though political competition has been more open and individual freedom greater in effectively functioning parliamentary democra-cies). It identifies democratic pluralism *per se* with one particular set of democratic institutions. In noting the defects of authoritarian regimes it tends to silence criticisms of the defects of representative democracy and liberal constitutionalism. In fact, the criticism of the one appears to validate the other, as if all alternatives had been covered in this opposition of totalitarianism and democracy. In Chapters 5 and 6 the defects of existing parliamentary democracy are considered and other forms of institutional framework are proposed to supplement it in promoting pluralistic political competition and an advanced liberal society.

The second reason why the central proposition of pluralism has been contested is that the basis of social difference in particular pluralist theories is often identified with specific forms of private property. Socialists have challenged the proposition because it appears to claim that private property, and therefore capitalism, is a necessary condition for political liberty. Socialists have, by and large, been more interested in proposing the collective ownership of the means of production than in seeking alternatives to capitalism in differentiated social ownership of these means. Unfortunately, the coming into being of socialist and social democratic regimes that have nationalized enterprises, services and forms of public provision has seemed to make the equation of private property and liberty plausible. Many ordinary people have found their bureaucratic entitlements less than satisfactory and their struggles with the agencies that provide them baffling and defeating. Two parallel confusions are going on here. Many pluralists do confuse the social basis of liberty with capitalistic private property. Many socialists confuse all private property with capitalism and refuse to accept cooperatives and other forms of social ownership as real alternatives to the state ownership of the means of production.

As one of the principal theorists of pluralistic democracy, R. A. Dahl, points out in his *A Preface to Economic Democracy* (1985), the equation of the objective of economic autonomy for large numbers of social agents with certain particular forms of private property is a *non sequitur*. This is particularly true when modern corporate property is included in the property rights defended and the whole bundle considered as if it conferred social autonomy and economic independence on most individuals. Which property rights are necessary to the liberty of the individual? Once one asks such a question then pluralist theory need no longer function as a bastion of the corporate capitalist order. The question necessarily raises the further one of the nature of the agents making economic decisions and the scope of those decisions. All economies involve a realm of differentiated decision-making agencies. As Chapter 2 argues, the idea of a single centralized agency elaborating a rational plan and therefore being the sole strategic source of economic decision-making is simply unrealizable. However, the differentiated agencies can be of very different characteristics and capacities. Big corporations may dominate the key decisions that are not made by large public bureaucracies. Individuals are then left with less central decisions, primarily those regarding consumption. Wider share ownership cannot resolve this question, for the one thing a 'share-owning democracy' *cannot* do is to give individual shareowners much influence or autonomy in economic decision-making. The more dispersed is the share ownership of a company the more likely is management control. Giving great freedom to corporations in their decision-making does not lead to the economic autonomy of large numbers of the people; rather it makes corporations politically influential and better able to pursue their own interests, whether or not these are in the public interest. Once the issue is posed in this manner then we can begin to consider pluralism in terms other than capitalistic apologetics. Pluralist theory is therefore compatible with the criticism of certain forms of private property and in particular of corporate capitalism. This is true not only of Dahl but of other modern critics of corporate capitalism like J. S. Coleman (1974) and also the more radical proponents of classical liberalism like J. S. Mill.

One danger in the radical pluralist critique of corporate business is the tendency to regard individuals as the sole legitimate social actors and the only real bearers of rights – Coleman (1974) certainly exemplifies this response. Organizations – and not all corporate entities are capitalist firms – cannot be treated as merely the sum of the actions of the individuals composing them nor can they be reduced to the benefits that they produce for individuals. In fact many activities require, and legitimately require, large continuing organizations having a corporate personality. Such organizations function as social actors and in consequence have distinct interests. It follows that such agents and interests must be recognized and involved in the polity. Democracy must involve other forms of representation than the election of representatives by popular vote. One argument to be found in Chapters 2, 4 and 5 of this book is that the existence of legitimate organizations having a corporate personality means that a 'corporatist' component is a necessary part of the reform and development of democracy. 'Corporatism' has received a very bad press but there is a good deal to be said for the direct representation of organized interests, as will be seen below. Such an argument goes beyond conventional versions of liberal democracy but it is compatible with the central proposition of pluralism outlined above, which makes no reference to specific institutional forms of representation and political competition.

Dahl (1985) argues that the pluralist thesis requires the economic autonomy of large numbers of social agents and does not require corporate property, which, on the contrary, leads to the subversion of that autonomy. Dahl proposes reforms that result in an economy in which the key decision-making units are workers' cooperatives. This, he contends, eliminates or radically reduces corporate power whilst maximizing the economic independence of individuals. But we should be wary of making the assumption that such autonomy in decision-making solves the economic and political problems in modern capitalism. An economy is not reducible to the enterprises of which it is composed, nor can we magic structural problems away by imagining that markets will perform all the tasks that intra-enterprise decision-making cannot accomplish or that such markets will lead to satisfactory outcomes for welfare and the economic autonomy of enterprises. Regulation of markets by public agencies and non-market provision on the basis of need of certain key services like health and education are essential if we are to have a society in which the bulk of agents enjoy minimum civilized standards of well-being and personal autonomy. After all, most people in an advanced industrial society will not be workers in industrial enterprises. As Chapter 2 contends, socialism – meaning the concern for equality and the provision of resources and services on the basis of need – will extend the scope and variety of state agencies and functions. This is so even in a system with extensive decentralization, worker-managed cooperative enterprises and markets for most industrial goods. Indeed, an economy with larger numbers of worker-owned and -managed enterprises will need extensive state regulation, planning, services and assistance – particularly if it has to compete in a world market where corporate enterprises still dominate.

(3)   A centralized, hierarchically organized and bureaucratic state is a bad partner for an economy of worker-managed independent enterprises. No one could imagine the prospects for political liberty to be very rosy in such a paradoxical situation. It is all too clear which of the components will dominate, as the example of Yugoslavia shows. This introduces the third sense of pluralism, for since the beginning of this century a current of thought has argued against the dominant conception of the modern sovereign state (that is, the one described by Max Weber and defended for its accuracy in Chapter 4). This current has argued that the state is not and cannot be the only

legitimate and independently existing entity in a polity apart from individuals. On the contrary, there are collective and corporate bodies, associations and lesser authorities, which are not merely the state's creatures. (The dominant theory of sovereignty regards such bodies as existing by the state's concession and as possessing by the state's fiat whatever conditional and revocable rights it chooses to endow them with.) It also follows that the state should not be conceived as a centralized and hierarchical agency in which sovereign authority emanates from a single centre; rather the state should be a complex of bodies, each possessing authority over some dimension of activity and having certain definite powers. This current draws its inspiration from the theory of associations of Otto von Gierke and can be found most elegantly expressed by J. N. Figgis in his *Churches in the Modern State* (1913).

This tendency has failed to win much support, for it has heretofore argued against the main tendency of the modern world – the growth of big government and the state's rigid defence of the theory of sovereignty as the basis of an unlimited right of regulation and intervention within its territory. The military–economic competition of states and the rise of a world divided into nation states has led to the relentless pursuit of control of all social activities by agencies of central government. Serious political and doctrinal opponents of this drive for control and assertion of absolute sovereignty have in consequence become 'internal enemies' for a wide variety of regimes. The Catholic Church has suffered particularly in this respect because it cannot accept the state's view of it as a mere licensed association among others. It has been persecuted for this reason by very diverse regimes: in Bismark's *Kulturkampf*, by the anti-clerical policy of Emile Combes in the French Third Republic, and by the Mexican revolutionary government in the 1930s. Trades unions have suffered in the same way and for the same reason, not simply because they are representatives of organized labour but because they have claimed to be autonomous organizations whose rights of action can never be merely whatever government chooses to give them in statute law.

It may be, however, that the ideas espoused by Figgis and by G. D. H. Cole and the guild socialists are now being favoured by circumstances and that the claims of the sovereign state are being discredited. Cole is taken seriously here, and there is a critical dialogue with him in Chapters 2, 4, 5 and 6 for precisely this reason. His early work and that of H. J. Laski offer one of the few sources of anti-statist and yet non-populist political theories available to the Left. Political problems are accumulating for which the centralized sovereign state offers no solution. In Europe, greater political integration has become a condition of the further economic development of the EEC and that integration evidently cannot take the form of the creation of a continental super-state. A complex federal and confederal solution, with distinct authorities organizing different dimensions of activity, is the only one possible. In Northern Ireland no programme of singular sovereign dominion will prevail against the inescapable fact of organically existing communities that attempt to use the current representative institutions to block any change not to their liking and will use force if that fails. As Boyle and Hadden (1985) demonstrate, the only possible solution is a complex confederal structure of authority.

It would be naive, however, to imagine that such forms can prevent intercommunal tension if there is not a sufficient political will to compromise, or that they can work well under conditions of militarization and intense international competition. The 'pluralist' argument for distinct levels and dimensions of authority, each with its own organic existence and particular functions, answers the question of how to combine the increasing scope and variety of public agencies and collectively exercised functions, which is the inescapable result of socialist policy, with the attempt to prevent authoritarian and inefficient bureaucratic centralism. But it has yet to prove it could do so in a world of superpower confrontation and corporate big business. Big government has been the product of fighting modern industrial wars, centralization has emerged from the requirements of social mobilization. The modern state has emerged as in part the creature and in part the controller of corporate big business. It centralizes decisions and collectivizes forms of provision. Much of this change has been promoted by socialists, but this is a 'socialism' almost nobody wants. 'Pluralism' in our third sense – and it is a rather different one from the first two senses – is taken seriously here but is recognized to have been advanced by people who paid little regard to the savage realities of political struggle and international competition.

(4)   The fourth sense of pluralism, 'antagonistic pluralism', is used here only in Chapter 4. It indicates an additional crucial component of pluralist theory, that an effective democracy depends on the commitment of most political actors to the norms of the democratic process. Northern Ireland today offers an example of antagonistic pluralist political competition and the Weimar Republic after 1928 another example. In both cases fundamentally antagonistic social and political forces use the framework of representative institutions to pursue their incompatible objectives and each is willing to go beyond that framework or to overthrow it if threatened by its continuance or if the objectives can better be attained by doing so. Social differences and the plurality of political forces that emerge from them are not always a factor conducive to democracy. Modern pluralist political theory (in senses 1 and 2) has clearly recognized this and has sought to specify the conditions of stable political competition. One such condition is the much criticized proposition that limited participation in and expectations of the political system promote stability and are a positive factor. The argument in defence of this proposition is that too extensive political participation on the part of the masses leads to demagogic forces capturing those actors who lack the competence, knowledge and resources to operate independently in politics.

This endorsement of limited participation and the dangers of mass politics stems from a misrecognition of the causes of antagonistic pluralism. These stem not from naive mass voters but from the major social interests and political forces pulling further and further apart so that they cease to occupy the same social and political world. These processes of divergence may either be communalist – each religious or ethnic group seeking autonomy for itself on its own terms, as is the case in Lebanon or Northern Ireland – or stem from radically divergent views of how the whole society should be organized proposed by political forces whose bases of support become increasingly exclusive and non-communicating, as happened in Weimar with the Nazis, Communists and Social Democrats.

Such radically divergent views of how the whole society should be organized are apparent in Britain, between the left of the Labour Party and the Thatcherites, and it is increasingly the case that political forces in Britain are divided regionally and socially into exclusive constituencies. Britain is not Weimar; but it is no longer, if it ever was, a country where either 'side' will tolerate the most radical programmes of the other. Both 'sides' are actually rather unpopular, but, however centrist majority opinion may be, the centrist political forces offer little prospect of dealing with the major social and economic problems. If economic circumstances further deteriorate and if political forces further polarize as a result, then British politics would be characterized by antagonistic pluralism. We also have our own equivalent of a 'problem' to which reactionary idiots may offer a 'final solution'. To reiterate, Britain is not Weimar but only an idiot of another type would imagine that it did not have the potential to become very like it.

It is idle to offer democratic socialism as the solution to this dilemma. It may well be. The problem consists not only in making enough people believe that – and want it – but in making many others who do not want it willing to accept it. If both these conditions are to be fulfilled, modern British socialism will have to acquire a viable political theory, a theory that spells out its commitment both to political change and to democracy. It has lacked anything resembling such a theory since the 1920s. In order to convince people that socialism and democracy are compatible, that people will not be regimented and silenced, we need to think and not to sloganize. Pragmatism accepts the political *status quo*; it must do because the existing political institutions and office are its sole reason for existence. If theorizing about political institutions is thought to be 'impractical', it will be left to those who are indeed impractical, to utopians. We need to convince not only our supporters but most of all our opponents that socialism does not mean in Max Weber's words an 'icy night' of bureaucratic darkness. If we don't, they will resist it to the death. Democratic socialism cannot be imposed gun-in-hand, it must therefore persuade enough of its enemies to permit it to exist. That is no easy task.

2 Law, Socialism and Rights

This chapter is the first of three concerned with the role of law in socialist states. It will consider three major problems:

(1) the question of 'civil liberties' under socialism – in practice, the conditions for securing forms of regulation, inspection and interdiction of the action of state agencies;
(2) whether the elimination of a certain legally sanctioned class of agents – 'private' owners of the means of production – problematizes the existence of the institution of 'law' itself;
(3) whether 'laws', whatever the political and economic system, must necessarily constitute subjects as possessive bearers of 'rights'.

The last problem links the two preceding: in Marxist theory the proprietal subject enjoying certain 'rights' is considered an irredeemably bourgeois notion, arising from the realities of individual private possession. While it is possible to argue that the notions of proprietal subject and possessive rights are in no sense specific to the organization of production in terms of commodity exchange, this point will be secondary in my argument. I shall argue that the notions of a given proprietal subject and of 'rights' are problematic categories in *any* legal system; that they create severe problems in securing the objectives towards which legislation is directed; and that attempting to solve questions of divergent interests in terms of 'rights' can only lead to impossible contradictions. This is because questions of 'rights' and of the priority of the 'rights' of one class of agents over another tend to generate doctrines that seek to necessitate the agent's possession of or priority to 'rights' by reference to its nature. These problems are in no sense specific to socialist states;

I shall illustrate them by reference to a salient example, the problems of abortion legislation in contemporary Britain.

The arguments advanced here challenge the theses of two leading legal theorists: in the Marxist camp E. B. Pashukanis, and in the liberal camp Ronald Dworkin. Both, by completely different methods and to different ends, argue that the subject endowed with rights is the vital element in law. Certainly it is a prominent component of legal ideologies, but, I would argue, one whose role must be minimized in the legal framework of any socialist state that seeks to avoid the abuses so evident in the USSR and minimized, whatever the dominant form of property law, in the resolution of certain complex dilemmas of social policy by means of law.

I shall begin with the second of the three major problems outlined above and, therefore, with the work of Pashukanis.

Law and Social Agents

Pashukanis (1979) attempted to establish a general theory of law based on Marxist method, a materialistic counter to bourgeois jurisprudence. In this theory law is explained as specific to, and as a necessary form of expression of, the relationships of commodity–capitalist society. In explaining law thus it is assigned a necessary content: law consists in the recognition, in the form of 'rights', of the realities of the possession of alienable things by individuals. Law is, in consequence, assigned a set of limits it cannot transgress, just as much as in theories that conceive the laws as embodying certain principles that are definitive of their nature (justice, equity, etc.). Pashukanis ends up adopting positions that have striking similarities to certain of the bourgeois theories whose method he repudiates. Law is for him, however, confined to the commodity form and will disappear along with that form.

I have criticized Pashukanis's work in *On Law and Ideology* (1979), but I must return to it because it is a direct and vigorous challenge to the enterprise of this chapter. The notion of a legal framework of a socialist state as something to be constructed and elaborated is for Pashukanis a nonsense; the work of socialists in respect of the law can only be its progressive deconstruction, the facilitation of its 'withering away'.

Pashukanis sets out in his theory to avoid the reduction of law to class interests. In doing so he posed two questions:

(1) What is the *form* of law, i.e. what is specific to and definitive of legal institutions?
(2) Why is the *legal*, rather than some other, form of regulation of social relationships necessary?

The answers he gives are less satisfactory than the questions. The form of law is defined by the categories of 'subject' and 'right': law consists in the recognition of the rights of subjects concerning possession. Law arises because it is necessary to the system of production that individual subjects be guaranteed full recompense on alienation of the fruits of their labours. Law is the means of regulating the social process of production, the connection of specialized individual private labours through the exchange of their products as commodities. Economic subjects are independent, linked only by mutual alienation of things, but also interdependent – they require that alienation in order to exist. Law resolves the antagonisms of this realm of differentiated individuals: law, the recognition by a supra-individual instance of their 'rights' to possession, is a condition of those individuals' relationships with one another. In these answers, law is equated with and confined to a certain conception of property rights and with commodity–capitalist social relations.

Pashukanis, therefore, conceives law as *recognizing* prior realities and *regulating* an already given realm of relations between agents. Recognition and regulation are necessary because of the specific problems of the relationships of autonomous and potentially antagonistic bourgeois individuals. This conception may be challenged in each of its elements, and yet it retains something of value. I have argued that it is by no means the case that the subjects 'recognized' and the activities regulated are given in their form prior to law, pointing to significant instances of the *construction* in legislation, and application, of categories of subject. Further, legal regulation is not confined to *antagonistic* relations between agents (questions of restitution, equity, etc.), or to agents of a particular form – human individuals as bearers of commodities. Regulation not only defines agents and imposes requirements of action on them;

it also establishes a relation between agents and the 'public power', not merely a relation between agents with the public power as adjudicator.

The value of Pashukanis's explanation of the form of law is that it sensitizes us to the problems posed by a realm of differentiated agents. Pashukanis supposes these agencies are human individuals (conceived as given social subjects) and that the form of their relationship is an exchange of commodities ('things'). But a realm of differentiated agencies of decision is in no sense limited to these forms. In order for such a realm to exist, the scope and limits of these agencies' actions must be defined and limited: this is a condition of their having a determinate capacity for decision. This is a matter not merely of *ordered* relations between these agencies (the classical 'problem of order' posits just such a realm of agencies with capacities for decision and asks how their actions can be made compatible; the 'problem' arises simply because the agents are made prior to their regulation), but of the existence of the agents in a determinate form. Agents are never *given*, be they tribal elders or the Factory Inspectorate. It is not merely a matter of making agents' actions *compatible* (such cannot be done by regulation); rather, it concerns the form of *definition* of the agents as agents. This necessarily arises whenever a realm of differentiated agencies of decision must be constituted, whether or not these agents are directly concerned with production, and *whether or not the relations between those agents take a commodity form.*

For Pashukanis, neither pre-capitalist nor socialist societies entail such realms of differentiated agencies of decision. Commodity production alone creates the necessity of regulating 'autonomous' individuals. In pre-capitalist societies, relations of personal dependence and hierarchy – subordination to the tribal community or the feudal lord – prevail, while in socialist societies centralized planned production expresses the conscious will of the associated producers. On the contrary, 'feudal' societies do involve differentiated agencies of decision, complexes of distinct organizations and public powers – monastic orders, urban corporations and guilds, barons and land-lords, etc. – and, certainly in England, elements of contractual relationships between landlord and tenant. The socialization of economic relations, as we shall see, cannot operate without differentiated agencies of decision. Laws and courts are a vital means of definition of the powers of feudal agencies, a power themselves and a means of regulation of disputes between agencies. Forms of legal regulation cannot be dispensed with under socialist forms of property.

Accepting for the time being this somewhat abstract notion of differentiated agencies of decision, I shall attempt to define the form of law in a way that does not limit law to one particular set of property rights or to the legal system of the 'bourgeois' states. Law is an instance of regulation: an institutionally specific complex of organizations and agents, discourses and practices, which operates to define (whether in codified rules or not) the form and limits of other organizations, agents and practices. Law, therefore, consists in the elements necessary to this instance:

(1) an apparatus of legislation: 'laws' issue from definite organizations advancing claims as to their scope and capacity (these *claims* differentiate laws as 'laws' from other classes of rule);

(2) rules produced by this apparatus defining the status and capacities of agents:

(a) the definition of these agents' *form of existence*, that is, the forms of organization and activity constructed as following from a legal personality (legal 'personalities' are differentiated; who or what is recognized as a person in one statute may not be recognized or may be recognized in a different form in another; legal persons such as limited companies, doctors, married women, etc., are complexes of statuses, powers and requirements imposed by various statutes);

(b) *norms of conduct* and requirements of regulation: these relate differentially to agents' statuses and to the realms of activity regulated (e.g. companies are required to file accounts, households to admit health visitors, etc.);

(3) an apparatus of adjudication in infractions and disputes, norms of conduct for its operations, and an apparatus to compel acceptance of the process of adjudication and its results.

Two qualifications need to be entered here. First, (1) and (2) are differentiated here but, given autonomy of decision in adjudication, the rules cannot remain unaffected by the process of their application; this applies no less where there is no 'common law' and a lesser role for precedent than in Anglo-Saxon courts. Second, there is no reason why the apparatus of enforcement should be institutionally separate from the legal agencies proper, as in the case of modern armies and police forces; before the development of these organizations, officers of the courts, bailiffs, etc., served to enforce judgment.

Pashukanis supposes a 'prior' realm of activity (production and exchange), given independently of its definition and regulation, which is homogeneous and inclusive and concerns a single category of agent (the proprietal subject). Each of the elements of this statement is challenged in the notion of a realm of differentiated agencies of decision subject to definition and regulation given above. First, it has been stressed that law does not necessarily consist in the recognition and expression of entities already existing outside it, 'organic' products of social life. Legislation and application are processes of the construction of agents and the organization of their existence through the form of a legal personality: I have argued this in respect of the limited company in *On Law and Ideology* (1979), and Jacques Donzelot in the *Policing of Families* (1980) demonstrates the construction of the mother as 'responsible agent of socialization' (a site of medicalized social superintendence distinct from the obligations of the 'wife') from the late nineteenth century onwards by legal rules and administrative practices concerned with social health legislation. Law (as an institutionally differentiated instance) cannot be the sole means of construction of agents. Various forms of administrative rules, practices and policies (state and semi-state; viz. the importance of 'private' charities in welfare provision and supervision in countries like Italy or Ireland) also serve in this direction, e.g. Board of Trade rules in respect of companies, DHSS rules in the case of mothers. These agencies are not, however, 'outside' the law: they are in turn differentiated agencies of decision constituted in a particular way in public law. Second, there is no homogeneous and inclusive realm of social life for law to express: Pashukanis conceives the essence of social relations as a *totality* of production and exchange; 'society' is a singular entity unified by its material life process. Social relations are conceived here not as a totality governed by a determinative principle, but as complexes of institutions, agents and activities that have no necessary unity, that permit of differentiation, divergence and non-intersection. Third, and following from this, all agents are not at par with one another, nor are they engaged in a single intersecting realm of activity: thus limited companies and mothers are both specific legal persons, but there is no identity of status or requirements of regulation and no necessary realm of contact between them.

Nothing differentiates 'laws' as such in the definitions given above from other classes of rule. Customs overseen by tribal elders and the rules of administrative bodies may equally well define agents and set norms of conduct. Village meetings and administrative tribunals may decide cases according to procedural rules just as courts do. Nothing differentiates laws, *as categories of rule*, from other forms of regulation of agents and their activities. What differentiates 'laws' are the claims in that regard made by the institutionally specific instances of regulation issuing and enforcing them.

Pashukanis's search for the 'form' of law, for the definitive features of its rules that would provide its *raison d'être*, was a chase after a chimera. It is legal *institutions* that differentiate the rules they make as 'laws'. Pashukanis's privileging of 'private law' was a profound error: law became an expression of social relationships, which required it and yet which determined how it met those requirements. Legislation and the form of legal institutions became a non-problem, a medium necessary to private law but one governed by its form. Challenging this organicist conception means taking the construction and application of particular laws by specific institutions within a framework of public law seriously. 'Laws' depend on the instance of regulation issuing them taking a definite public form, as bodies within the legal framework of a state.

Laws are effective *as laws* precisely because they are the products of certain institutions presented as a sovereign public power and because specific state agencies and practices pursue their enforcement. The regulatory instance has a specific form as a complex of institutions and has political conditions of existence of its operation and effectivity. These institutional and political conditions of legislation and application have specific effects on the rules that can be passed and enforced; these conditions are not some neutral medium for the 'expression' of prior and determining social needs. Public law is thus central to 'law' in two senses. First, it is the condition for the differentiation of 'law' from other categories of definitive/regulatory rules – the creation of an institutionally specific instance of regulation as a public power. Second, in order that public power of regulation is itself regulated, definite limits of scope and action are placed on legal institutions.

I have argued that rules of definition and regulation are conditions of existence for a realm of differentiated agencies of decision; this requires a regulatory instance. Further, I have argued that a condition of existence of 'law' is an institutionally specific instance of regulation, which is itself presented in the form of public law. I shall now attempt to link these two propositions systematically.

A realm of differentiated agencies of decision is an abstraction that implies:

(1) that a definite sphere of activity (production, distribution, war, cultural propagation, etc.) requires to be organized in the form of a number of distinct agencies (whether this be due to limits of information, control techniques, division of labour, geographical division is not pertinent here); these agencies may perform the activity in series or in combination;

(2) that the agent is a unit of organization of the activity; the agent's actions, however much circumscribed by conditioning factors, are determined in their form by calculation and not given to them by some other agent. The classic examples of such agents are capitalist firms, but others are just as pertinent, like monastic orders deciding whether and where to establish a new house, or feudal landlords deciding to establish a local market or to use fines more systematically, or the leadership of an autonomous expeditionary corps determining what strategy to pursue;

(3) that the agent operates in a sphere of activity in parallel with, opposed to or in combination with other organizing agents; thus feudal landlords may hold manors in the same village, or socialist enterprises may recruit labour in the same locality or perform services for one another, etc.

The assignation of status and the imposition of norms of conduct are a condition of the agent's action in that they set it definite forms and limits. This makes definite forms of calculation and organization possible, even if those involve breaching the limits; a feudal landlord bent on increasing the scope of fines has a set of instances of their use and a calculation of the possible. Definatory and regulatory rules are a form of construction of agents or organizational design. These rules are not merely 'legal'; for example, the rules of a monastic order for the regulation of houses serve as a plan for new establishments as well as for the conduct of existing ones. But 'laws' (rules issued by institutions making certain claims) serve an analogous function: laws construct the *form of existence* of subjects and organizations as agents in definite arenas (feudal tenant, on the one hand, juryman and keeper of the peace, on the other; mother as agent of socialization, wife as bearer of certain property rights, etc.). Laws and administrative rules coordinate the action of agencies, producing means of cooperation, reconciliation and control. Coordination of the interaction of agencies depends in the first instance on the delimitation of their permitted form and the field of their action. Legislation constitutes agents in setting limits and prescribing norms of conduct, and in that way is 'regulative' in a more basic sense than any policing or settling of disputes.

In order to define and regulate a realm of agents, the instance of regulation in question must be presented as external to each of the agents and 'superior' to them. It cannot without difficulty be an agent at par with them and perform this regulatory function. If that were the case, then one agent would define the form of existence and terms of conduct of the other agents in an activity in which it was involved. This would tend either to decompose the differentiated nature of the realm by compromising the autonomy of the other agents, or, to the extent that the definatory agent operated on the principle of *primus inter pares*, it would subject its own operations to its own rules, and thereby tend to differentiate itself into a regulatory and an operational instance. Regulation requires a specific agency which is not at par with those to be regulated.

There is no reason why, for any given activity, this instance should take the form of a state or a single dominant public power. For the regulation of definite spheres of activity other forms are possible: governing councils, trade associations, agreed arbitrators, etc. Nor does the invocation of the 'state' resolve all difficulties. However much it may be *presented* as a single public power, the 'state' is itself a complex of differentiated agencies of decision: ministries, local councils, specialist bodies, etc. *As an assemblage of organizations it stands as much in need of definition and regulation as any other realm of agents.* Public law serves this regulatory function by defining the component parts of the 'state' as agencies of decision with definite powers and spheres of activity; as a specific instance it reviews and regulates the actions of those state agencies.

As such, law is at once definitive *of* the state and at the same time a complex of institutions *within* it; as a regulatory instance it is a mere portion of the state's agencies and activity. The state cannot be explained by the legal forms in which it is presented, or by the requirement to define and regulate spheres of activity. Further, as we have seen, the legal characterization of the state as a single public power is at variance with its being a realm of distinct agencies of decision, and this realm raises all the problems of control and regulation any other would. Our discussion will not lead us down the slippery slope to 'state derivationism' or to conceiving state apparatuses as exhausted in their character and action by the forms of their presentation in public law.

For all the qualifications and limits to a legal analysis of state apparatuses, public law is a vital component of the state: it establishes the formal limits and scope of state power, the conditions of access to and the means of its exercise. The role of public law may be schematized as follows:

(1) the definition of the component elements of the state and their 'powers' – a *constitution* (organizational design – legal form of existence);
(2) through the legislative, applicatory and adjudicative elements thus defined, the definition of the status and capacities of non–state entities.

Public law involves the 'fiction' that the state exists in the form of law and that law is not merely one definite sphere of state activity but is definitive of the whole. Public law as outlined above is no peculiarity of 'capitalist' states; feudal states, the Roman Republic, the USSR, all had or have constitutions and participate in this 'fiction'.

The very notion of 'law' as an institutionally distinct and superior category of rules is implicated in this 'fiction'; that is, the legal instance is not a member of the classes of agents it regulates (it is not an agent at par with others), and yet it is subject to itself; it is not outside or above the rules of law. Law is always the product of specific agencies of decision and yet is supposed to be subordinate to itself. This 'fiction' is a condition of its action: it *is* a fiction (1) because laws and regulatory instances are not a homogeneous sphere of legality (Law) – there is no 'Law' in general, only specific bodies of rules and definite apparatuses regulating particular spheres of activity (there is no necessity for these bodies' categories and practice to form a coherent system); (2) because the rules of procedure that legal agencies follow are specific constructions of other agencies of decision, legislatures and higher courts. The notion of a 'rule of Law' embodies this fiction – that legislatives and higher courts are themselves bound by procedural rules. It is a doctrine that unifies the complex of rules and agencies into a single entity, 'Law'; this unification serves as the ground of certain claims, for example that *all* laws are equally valid and should be obeyed.[1] Laws *always* have an 'outside': laws and procedural rules are subject to transformation by definite agencies (legislatures, Supreme Court, etc.).

In public law this 'fiction' – whereby the 'outside' is placed within the law – is presented in the doctrine of 'sovereignty'. The sovereign is the source of law and procedural rules: state and legal agencies represent (are delegated portions of) the sovereign power. The doctrine of sovereignty transcends different forms of state and constitution; it is in no sense alien to feudal constitutions, retained and reinforced by the doctrines of the liberal era, and, as we shall see, its analogues affect profoundly Marxist conceptions of the socialist state.

I have contended that state apparatuses and practices are not reducible in their practices and effects to law or in their action to the limits of their own legal form. Public law constructs administration and state activity as a realm of differential agencies of decision, agencies that it purports to define and regulate. But it cannot subsume them, precisely because they must be assigned a definite autonomy of action in order that the state's activities be organized. The very legal definition of state agencies necessarily poses the problem of 'control' of administrative agencies: legal agencies define capacities that they do not exercise. The very notion of a limit imposed by regulation implies an agency capable of exceeding it and not subsumed as part of the regulatory instance. The very notions of 'constitutionality' and 'rule of law' are symptoms of this problem: legislative and adjudicative agencies are merely one portion of the complex of agencies and practices that exist within the constitutional confines of the public domain; they are a necessary part but in no sense necessarily primary, as constitutional doctrines assert.

The state as a realm of differentiated agencies of decision is a problematic notion. The limits of and conditions of access to the public domain are set by laws, but the realm of agencies thus established is 'policed' by definite agencies with limited capacities of supervision and control. Access to and operation of 'public' agencies is necessarily problematic: the doctrines of 'constitutionality' and 'rule of law' attempt to cover this paradox, and serve as claims to intervention and review by particular state agencies (select committees, higher courts, etc.). The paradox is doubled in that the agencies closest to being definitive of the constitution (the limits of public power, whether formalized and codified or not) have the greatest capacity (in the formal claims of the public law) to transform it. Constitutional doctrines and the form of legislative agencies therefore can be matters of political consequence; the 'fiction' is not an illusion despite its paradoxical and problematic nature. The notorious Article 48 of the Weimar Constitution is an example. Public law and legal agencies are not above politics (even if such claims are advanced for the impartiality of higher courts' functions of review), but they can be an independent factor in it, depending on the complex of political conditions. Constitutional courts can set limits and serve as a vital factor in politics (a factor with conditions in other political agencies' support of these institutions' practice), as the example of Chile shows: Allende's government could be formed as a parliamentary and elected administration only on conditions set by the Electoral College and the courts.

The state is given coherence and limits in the legal form of a constitution; as a doctrine of delegated powers this defines away the problem of the state as a complex organization of differentiated and interacting agencies of decision. 'Sovereignty' defines the state as a homogeneous space of realization of the will of the sovereign subject (monarch, people-in-representation). 'Sovereignty' as a constitutional category serves a dual function:

(1) It resolves in doctrine the paradox involved in the notion of 'law' (an institutionally specific instance of regulation advancing claims); that is how 'law' (legal agencies) can at once be 'above' the activities it regulates, and yet subject itself: law is the

will of the sovereign appropriately expressed – the sovereign because sovereign is competent to make law and set its procedures.

(2) It therefore serves ideologically to prioritize certain agencies and activities within the apparatuses of state; these are held to express the 'will' of the sovereign, as for example with Parliament.

Doctrines of 'sovereignty' construct the state in the form of a hierarchy of expression of the sovereign will. The state can thus be thought of as and held to be a single, homogenized and hierarchized medium of a will that emanates from its centre. This notion of a centre as a subject with a will is a 'fiction' no less than the notion of law as subject to itself. As a consequence of this 'fiction', certain agencies are presented as having more power than others.

Law and public law cannot be separated; this is because what differentiates 'law' from other classes of rule are the claims advanced by institutionally specific instances of regulation. I have dwelt here on the 'fictions' involved in making those claims; law and doctrines of the nature of the public power cannot easily be separated. Definition and regulation – establishing the form of existence, scope and limits of action of 'its' agencies – are necessary to *any* form of state. The question I shall consider later is whether the doctrines of 'rule of law' and 'sovereignty' can serve any constructive purpose in resolving problems of the organization of socialist states, in particular the problem of securing the effects of 'civil liberties'. The difficulty as we can see already is that problems of 'policing' state apparatuses are *not* removed by a framework of public law, by doctrines of 'rule of law', 'sovereignty' or 'rights of the citizen'. All states, as complexes of agencies of decision, *must* take a public law form. The USSR is no exception. It will be argued that both the notions of a 'withering away of law' and of 'socialist legality' are equally problematic. The invocation of 'legality' and the call for its abolition are *parallel* responses and are not the answer to the problem.

LAW AND SOCIALISM

Pashukanis is consistent and rigorous in his supposition that law is confined to commodity–capitalist relations. His conception of law is consistent with the central tenet of Marxist political theory – that socialism is a transitional phase in which the state 'withers away'. The objectives of socialist construction are twofold: the formation of a planned economy, and the deconstruction of state power arising from class antagonism. Since law arises from the necessities of commodity production, private law will disappear with private production. The legitimation of the repressive apparatus of the state in the form of law (derived from analogies with private law) will disappear with the abolition of class exploitation and class struggle.

The condition for this 'withering away of law' is the elimination of commodity production and with it the *necessity of differentiated agencies of decision* ('private' property = individuals separated from one another acting as agents of production and exchange). This elimination of differentiated agencies of decision is consistent with the Marxist conception of socialism:

(1) Planned production replaces the circulation of commodities; distinct units of production become mere technical necessities rather than economic agents – *the plan is the centralization of economic decisions*;

(2) The plan is the economic expression of popular democracy: the specialized administrative agencies and institutions of the 'bourgeois' state (a public power 'separated' from the people) will disappear and are replaced by popular democratic, legislative–executive bodies that are the direct expression of the popular will (soviets, commune state).

Retained in Marxist political theory are analogues of the categories of 'sovereignty' and 'general will': popular democracy is the means of action of the people-as-sovereign. The representative bodies of bourgeois democracy are rejected in favour of a doctrine of direct representation of the masses (the notion of 'people' remains central *despite classes*; the organized working class are conceived as the representatives/leaders of the whole people, the 'vanguard' that represents the objective interests of the masses as a whole). Popular democracy depends on a concept of representation of the 'general will' through the politically active working class and on a notion that power resides in the people, that they alone by their own self-action can organize their own emancipation. The transitional state has its own doctrine of legitimation that counters and parallels bourgeois conceptions of 'sovereignty'. Marxist political theory rejects the administrative centralization of the 'bourgeois' state, the concentration of capacities in distinct agencies to which access is limited. It stresses, however, the centralization of decisions: planning can work only by concentrating resources and decisions in a single centre; this is possible because the people (acting through a complex of bodies – soviets, communes) are capable of formulating a general set of interests that reflects their fundamental unity. The plan can be centralized and democratic because, ultimately – in spite of clashes and contradictions – the people are one agency of decision, a unity with a single interest.

This notion of the elimination of distinct agencies of decision haunts Marxist political theory: Lenin and Mao stumbled and staggered away from it in their attempts to cope with the organizational problems of socialist states, but they never broke with – indeed, they further enhanced the importance of[2] – the notion of the people as a unitary agency of decision. This unity rested on common objective interests that the masses, given the means and the time to overcome obstacles, could not but express.

Leninist socialism has been criticized from the 'Left' and the 'Right' in an attempt to account for and seek means to overcome what is considered to be the particular problem of the phenomenon of 'Stalinism'.

Trotskyists have predominated in formulating the main lines of 'left' criticism. This has sought to find the sources of Stalinism in the two elements of political organization absent from Marx's *Civil War in France* (1871): political parties and the retention of the centralized state administration. Thus the critique of 'substitutionalism' stresses the danger of the vanguard party – that the party isolates itself from the self-action of the working class and the leadership of the party is in consequence able to bureaucratize and subordinate the party apparatus. Parallel to this is the failure to 'smash' the state, the retention of bourgeois institutions and bureaucratic personnel separated from the people. Often these criticisms are traced to the backwardness of the economic and political development of Russia: the weakness of the working class and the absence of a developed centralized economy made bureaucratic organization necessary. These criticisms give further weight to the notion of popular

sovereignty: a developed economy and working class will make a
non-repressive centralized system possible; it will homogenize the
'people' (drawing them into industrial production and wage labour)
and make them capable of united autonomous action. Planned production without repression will be possible because the objective
basis of contradictory interests has been eliminated and the means for
democratic mass decision will be created.

The problem with these critiques is that in them parties and states
are thought of as at best regrettable necessities imposed by the
conditions of fighting the 'old society'. They are deformations of the
'self-emancipation of the working class'. The whole political
content of socialism is here predicated on the notion of a unitary
'working class' (as representative of the people) capable of realizing
its 'interests' in mass action if not held back or sold out by its own
leadership. This predication is nothing but a disaster: classes cannot
be political actors, and 'interests' – political objectives – are not given.
Political struggle *always* takes the form of definite organizations with
formulated programmes operating in particular institutional/
political conditions. These organizations may make claims to
represent classes, but they are not classes: the specific form of their
organization is not derived from classes, but is a matter of available
institutional forms and means of construction. The SPD (the
German Socialist Party) was a mass electoral party conditioned by
the voting system and conditions of struggle; it succeeded *because* it
organized and competed in national elections, *not* because of its
doctrines or claims of representativeness (other German groups also
claiming to be socialist and to embody the 'interests' of the working
class failed to do this). Again, the soviets were definite institutions,
with definite personnel and limited organizational capacities, *not* the
'people' in action. Kautsky saw this clearly when he defended the
specificity of political organization against the economistic doctrines
in the early 1900s, and again in *The Dictatorship of the Proletariat* (1918)
when he argued – *against* Lenin (who had adopted Kautsky's earlier
position) – that while classes may 'rule' (whatever that means)[3] they
cannot 'govern'. Socialism must mean the organization of politics by
parties, and of government (specific capacities of control and
decision) by state and other agencies.

The critique of Stalinism from the 'Right' accepts that questions of
the form of organization of the socialist state cannot be resolved by

the supposition of a popular 'will' prior to and independent of them which they must express. The 'rightist' critique has followed two lines:

(1) *Of the problems of planning.* It is impossible to centralize all decisions concerning the utilization of productive resources and their distribution in a single agency. This involves decentralized decision-making by enterprises and other organizations (welfare agencies, etc.). This critique, stressing the problems of information and span of control, has been primarily formulated by 'market socialists' (Brus, Sik, etc.), but the critical point being made here with great force is not confined to meeting the difficulties of control through market allocation and monetary calculation. The necessity of differentiated agencies of decision (enterprises, etc.) remains even if their relationships do not take the form of monetary exchange.

(2) *Of the problems of authoritarianism.* This confronts the problem of organizing state activities in such a way that elementary 'civil liberties' – freedom of correspondence, association, right of criticism – are not violated. This is seen in terms of limiting the prerogatives of the central party apparatus, the political police and so on. Two main lines of response predominate: calling for the restoration of 'socialist legality', the implementation of the violated formal rules of institutions like the party, respecting the provisions of the Soviet constitution, etc., or reintroducing 'pluralism', as in the various Eurocommunist strategies. These criticisms have serious defects but they do pose definite problems of organization as specific issues to be resolved at their own level. First, the forms of institutional organization of the economy (how enterprises relate to one another and to state agencies): it is recognized here that the apparatuses of control and decision-making are not given as some necessary 'expression' of the basic production relations. Second, how the imposition of a definite scope and set of limits on state agencies' actions can be assured: this too demands specific organizational means.

Classical Marxism has resolutely refused to think through such questions of organization because it has refused them autonomy.

Socialism's structure is a matter of the effects of the basic relations of production and the conditions of class struggle. The resolution of political problems is located in the, ultimate, unity of action and interests of the working class. The discussion of the specific forms of institutions, organizational practices and legislation cannot anticipate this dialectic. To do so is to fall into the illusions of rationalism. Socialism is a transitional phase of social relations, the period of the 'transition to communism'. It is governed by the necessities of the class struggle and of transforming social relations. The one necessity makes all questions of organization conjunctural; institutions, laws, etc., can have no fixed form but depend on the needs of the struggle and the creativity of the leadership and masses in responding to them. The other necessity makes limits to mass and state action unthinkable; nothing that preserves the capacities of the bourgeois class or impedes the transformation of social relations can be permitted. Under communism, questions of organization will cease to be *political*. Organization is a matter of the 'administration of things', of socially neutral and consensual technique. Relations of production cease to be constraints because they are nothing but the conscious and rational direction of society to the fulfilment of its material needs. These needs and interests are unproblematic because they are the expression of a single popular will. This rejection of the 'rationalism' of attempting to determine the organizational problems and requirements of 'socialist' states is made in the interests of a 'realism'. But this realism is a curious hybrid. On the one hand, it is a scientism: socialist social relations are an effect of the basic determinants of material production and class struggle. The 'realism' depends on a certain causal doctrine that treats socialism as a totality governed by its determinative principle. On the other hand, in order that the categories of this scientism be sustained, it involves notions of a popular 'general will' and of communist society as governed by the teleology of a communal rationality. These notions are the value stances that underlie Marxism's pretensions to 'realism', and are the conditions of socialism's objective evolution into a desirable form of society. They are, moreover, not demonstrable by this scientism, if as is claimed the construction of socialism is an objective process whose form and course cannot be predicted. But it is only an 'objective process', compatible with the objectives of Marxist political theory, if it gives rise to a *subject* capable of making the process 'its' conscious collective action. The supposition of this subject is no more 'realistic' than the notion that specific processes of organizational construction are both possible and necessary.

This latter supposition rests on the conception of social relations as something other than a totality governed by a determinative principle. It accepts the specificity and potential discontinuity of social relations. It does not involve the acceptance of the notion that social relations can be merely legislated for, that there are no constraints; rather, it involves the analysis of organizational construction as a means of overcoming constraints. This conception of social relations is no novelty (although its capacity for self-defence against orthodox Marxism is). G. D. H. Cole in his *Social Theory* (1921) conceived social relations as a specific complex of 'associations' with no given form and with no necessary interrelationships. Cole, at the time a non-Marxist socialist, took the question of the specific forms of organization of socialist social relations seriously. *Guild Socialism Re-Stated* (Cole, 1920) is a blueprint for institutional design. Cole based his theory on a critique of the concept of 'representation' (a challenge to the Webbs' schemes for a Socialist Commonwealth with a plurality of representative institutions). Representative bodies can never 'represent' the diverse wills and personalities of their individual electors – representation is merely a mechanism of providing the personnel of certain bodies. This critique of representative democracy as a principle of organization is not made in the service of a doctrine of popular democracy. There is no concept of the 'people' as a unity or 'sovereignty' in Cole's political theory. These categories involve the problematic notions of a 'general will', or of will-in-delegation, which are no less problematic than the conception of the representation of individual wills through elective mechanisms. Cole styled his political theory 'functional democracy'. 'Associations' are definite bodies established to administer or pursue a particular activity (sport, sociability, production, cooperative consumption); they are freely entered into by members. Suffrage was to be based on *activity*: an individual had as many votes as associations and as much say as his involvement. Members of associations would be assigned to collaborative bodies to pursue the business of their mutual cooperation.

The classic criticism of Cole's guild socialism is that it ignores the general problem of coordination of these associations and, therefore, the need for a central instance of coordination, the state.[4] To the extent that it recognizes this problem, its solution restores the state in all but name. This criticism is correct as far as it goes, but it supposes that the answer to a plurality of associations lies in the *centralization* of force and economic decision-making. This very centralization generates a plurality of differentiated agencies of decision, which pose problems no less acute than a plurality of associations freely entered into. The critics are correct that Cole's merely *ad hoc* and consultative conception of the coordination of the activities of a complex of interacting associations is inadequate. But why? First, there are requirements of information and division of labour that necessitate continual coordination, not a constant process of *ad hoc* adjustment. But these are no better handled by the notion of a single centre rather than a centreless plurality. There can be no *general* solution to the questions of information collection and relay, of techniques of control, etc. Second, what all questions of organization involving a plurality of associations or agencies generate are the problems of the definition of their form and the regulation of their action in the form of limits. Associations *cannot* be coordinated if no limits are placed on their competencies and actions: the absence of such limits generates a plurality of agencies of decision limited only by their own objectives, dependent on each other's compliance and goodwill as to the areas in which the respective decisions of each pertain. The absence of imposed limits inhibits organizations' calculation and the performance of definite tasks; the result would be competition for resources and multiple performance of functions.

Cole proposes a realm of differentiated agencies of decision. Such a realm, as we have seen, requires a regulatory instance that imposes limits in the sense of requirements placed on agents by the definition of their *forms of existence* (status, scope and capacities of action) and *norms of conduct*. The regulatory instance serves as a mechanism of organizational design and supervision. It does not and cannot solve all the problems of the coordination and control of a realm of differentiated agencies of decision; it does make such a realm possible and, therefore, the appearance of *definite* rather than *generalized* problems of control of, coordination of and interaction between the agencies. This differentiation/limitation of agencies must have a locus of decision not at par with the agencies but 'above' them. This locus – to be capable of effects – must be independent of any of the agencies to be regulated and must have a capacity to enforce limits upon them. This general support can only have the form of a 'public power': a specific instance of regulation advancing claims in this regard. Cole's associationalism indicates why. *All* agencies that interact must be assigned limits and brought into definite relations; the regulatory instance must have a scope adequate to the realms of agencies in question. The regulatory instance must itself take a definite form, assign limits to its action, and resolve (in definition) the problem of itself as a realm of differentiated agencies.

Posed in this problem of 'coordination' set by Cole's plurality of autonomous but interacting associations is the necessity of some form of 'constitution', in the sense of an organizational design and certain conditions of its regulatory maintenance. An instance of regulation, itself definite and limited, is nothing less than a framework of public law. Law, as we have seen, is *not* the entirety of the state; it is the regulatory instance that defines the public domain and agents in general. Which agencies and activities are part of the state as a legal unity cannot be specified in general. A framework of public law is *not* a solution to all the problems of coordination and control of state or other agencies, nor does it have a general definite content or effectivity. It can be made to have definite effectivities as part of the overall design and setting of the conditions of action of state and other agencies.

To recapitulate, a constitution is the definition of the entities in the 'public' domain, their capacities and limits of action vis-à-vis one another and other agents. The 'state' always entails a set of differentiated agencies, with capacities to dispose of resources and make decisions in respect of spheres of activity: it therefore entails a regulatory instance. *Socialist states, by increasing the scope and variety of state agencies and functions, accentuate rather than reduce the need for an effective framework of public law to regulate the 'public' domain and its relations with other agents.*

Existing socialist societies are not without a framework of public law. The definition of state property, the form of enterprises, state agencies and so on necessitates this. The USSR and the People's Republic of China both now boast constitutions; the former has a developed apparatus of administrative law and courts. The weakness of these constitutions is not their absence; constitutional documents and legal institutions are just as present in the USSR as they are in the

USA. Law is neither inoperative nor systematically 'violated', but limited in its role. It is not a question of 'arbitrariness', of power without legal definition. Kirchheimer in *Political Justice* (1961) explains the failure of legal regulation of the actions of state agencies and the non-institutionalization of 'civil liberties' or political rights in the Eastern bloc. He does so without falling into the crudities of the conventional concept of 'totalitarianism', of an unlimited and arbitrary state. What he stresses is that the legislative and adjudicative instances exist and function – they define state property, make rules, try criminal cases, etc. – but that they lack, as institutions, autonomy as political agencies in decision-making. Thus the Soviet or GDR constitution and state organization are not constructed *in order to* attempt to limit, inspect, supervise and control the actions of certain crucial state agencies. In his examination of the GDR he takes full account of the fact that there are competent legal specialists, that 'due process' is followed and so on. The crucial point is that the courts are part of an administrative hierarchy and are directly subject in their adjudicative decisions to orders from, interventions by and more subtle pressures emanating from the Ministry of Justice. A similar point can be made about legislation: the Supreme Soviet in the USSR does not function as an autonomous political body setting norms for and reviewing the conduct of the state administration and party. This is not merely because the party manipulates the election of candidates, or because opposition is subject to police measures. There is no conception of or room in official Soviet ideology for the differentiation of political functions in such a way that the higher levels of state and party decision-making be subject to limit and review. Without this differentiation, without political autonomy of the legislative and adjudicative agencies, the 'rule of law' or 'socialist legality' means very little. In fact, the repression of the opposition in the contemporary USSR is generally by legally defined and sanctioned institutions and means: dissidents are tried under rules and sentenced by the courts; the police, frontier guards and prisons are institutions established in public law; and even the incarceration of dissidents in mental hospitals works through the decisions of legally specified agents (doctors and psychiatrists) with the power of assessing grounds for committal.

The current Soviet state is hardly the ideal of most sections of the Left, a few hardened 'Marxist–Leninist' ultras apart. But the Left, in the interest of attaining a radical and complete transformation of social relations, is if anything even less committed to constructing legal and organizational limits to state and mass actions. Without such limits, which if effective must create bases for opposition and obstacles to change, all references to 'rights' of opposition, criticism, etc., are pious cant. The 1936 Constitution included an impressive collection of 'rights' of the citizen, but no specification of the mechanisms of enforcement that would make these 'rights' practical capacities. The 1977 document is little better in this respect. It is not a matter of individuals being endowed with 'rights' in the abstract, but of agencies being capable of limiting the practices of others.[5] The problem is the absence of institutions to defend certain agents' capacities for action and to limit those of others. In large part these institutions must be legislative and adjudicative agencies; to be effective these agencies require differentiated capacities for enforcement (their own police powers, review bodies and inspectorates) and an ideological commitment of political leaders and the mass of citizens to such forms of regulation. There is virtually no place for such commitment in the classical forms of Marxist political theory. Courts, specialist review bodies, supervision by legislature, administrative police, etc., are hardly institutions to commend themselves to Marxists. Yet these and others like them are none the less necessary if public discussion of, criticism of and opposition to the policies of socialist state agencies are to be possible. Such freedom of criticism and opposition, like the legal regulation necessary to support it, is not something alien to socialism, a concession to liberal 'pluralism'; it is a constituent part of any conception of a viable socialist state.

'Socialization' – the conversion of activities and resources to a public or communal property form, the administration and distribution of activities and resources in non-commodity forms – extends the 'public' sphere, the scope and capacities of state and cooperative agencies. To the extent that it does so it increases the complexity of the public domain and the need for regulation. 'Socialization' is not an automatic process, nor are its forms of organization and objectives given by basic property and economic relations. 'Socialization' must create, for this very reason, accentuated problems of differences of policy line and objectives, and clashes between specific 'interests' within the institutions of state and among organized bodies of citizens. Unless these differences can be openly expressed and discussed, the prospects for effective, lasting and

practical resolutions of such questions of organization and policy are dismal. Freedom of criticism is not a 'concession' to avoid certain unpleasant consequences; it is before all else a condition of efficiency in administration. Free discussion itself cannot, however, resolve severe clashes of organized interests: it is absurd to suppose a dialectic of reason or a spontaneous process of compromise. Policy decisions must take place according to procedures, which include means for resolving 'hard cases' and subjecting decisions to review. These procedures must inevitably mean assigning legislative and adjudicative bodies a central place in policy inspection and review: it is only by developing and extending means to permit serious examination of alternatives according to rules of procedure that socialist states can make any claims to advances in political organization over 'capitalist democracies' like the USA or Sweden.

I shall now consider in more detail how and why the alternative Marxist conception of the solution to the problem of policy-making and regulation of state agencies – 'popular democracy' – cannot function, *on its own*, as an effective means of legislation, inspection and control.

Legislative bodies are necessary to any instance of regulation; they are a condition for defining agents and limiting their action in the form of rules. These rules are not a formality, but must be adjusted to serve certain objectives and conditions of practicality. In consequence these bodies must be composed of personnel with competence and information to make rules relevant and workable. This requires cognizance of different forms of agents and their conditions of action. These bodies require an ideological commitment to the process of regulation on the part of members and other agents, a style of deliberation that is not limited by other agencies and bodies.

These remarks are not made in order to impose a model of parliamentary or representative democracy on socialist social relations. The effectiveness of legislative bodies cannot be assessed in terms of their 'representativeness', in the sense of purporting to represent the wills or interests of a constituency from which is derived the mandate or membership of the body. Ironically, doctrines of parliamentary and popular democracy both involve this concept of 'representation': it serves to legitimate the claim of legislative bodies to be 'sovereign', unlimited in their right to make rules because they are authentic expressions of majority will.

Democracy is often identified with 'representativeness'. But 'democracy', in the sense of electing the membership of legislative bodies (whether directly as with Parliament or indirectly in the case of half of the delegates to the Supreme Soviet), is *a mechanism for the provision of a personnel*. This objective is served, and is no more or less 'representative', if 20 per cent of the electorate vote in order to do this (as in some UK local government elections) or over 90 per cent (as in elections in the Soviet Union). Voting does not mean endorsement of the policies (if any) advocated by parties and candidates (this is blatantly obvious in the USSR, but occurs elsewhere; voting studies – however problematic – have shown that preference bears no necessary relation to support of party policies). Measuring the effectiveness of democratic mechanisms as 'representation' depends on a conception of what the 'interests' to be represented are, and of necessity the only way of measuring this effectiveness is to use *some other mechanism of representation of interests* (opinion polls, local committees, referenda or whatever). The circle of 'representation' can never be closed, however much it is doubled by other representative mechanisms and measures. Democracy – forms of election – must be assessed as a way of providing personnel for bodies and the work those personnel do, and not in terms of some doctrine of the 'representation' by those personnel of the interests of some constituency.

The personnel of a legislative body need not be at par with one another in status or arrive by the same mechanism – a point that will be elaborated later. We are conditioned by doctrines of parliamentary and popular democracy to suppose that the membership of legislative bodies should be homogeneous and equal in status, all alike in being representatives of their constituents. This derives from the notion that there is a sovereign subject to be represented, the 'people', and each component member of this subject is equal to any other. Each representative of the members must therefore be equal to any other. But legislatures have included and do include members of different status and routes of arrival: the House of Lords or the Business and Universities votes before 1947 are examples in the UK; the USSR has its Soviet of Nationalities; while feudal parliaments were characteristically divided into 'estates'. This may appear an absurd pedantry, but membership must be dictated by considerations of effectiveness in producing workable rules. This may demand a diverse personnel with different roles, as sources of information, rapporteurs to other decision-making agencies, etc. Personnel are homogenized by the notion of a sovereign and unitary constituency whose interests must be represented. There is no such given constituency.

The personnel to be provided and the mechanism of their provision are to be determined by the objectives of the legislative body. In this case they are twofold and the conditions of their attainment are twofold also. The first objective is to supervise a complex of agencies of decision (enterprises, ministries, parties, etc.) in order to make forms of their coordination and interaction possible. The second is to supervise certain of these agencies (police, political parties, etc.) in order to inhibit certain consequences – suppression of opposition and criticism in particular. The first condition is that the supervisory body must have a definite autonomy from the agencies it must inhibit (ministries, parties, police). This cannot be achieved merely by enunciating a doctrine of the 'separation of powers'; legislative bodies may indeed need to inquire more closely into administrative activities than the conventions of such doctrines would envisage. The second condition is that those bodies have the capacity to deal with complex administrative and organizational problems by means of rules in a way that is both practical and directed toward the political objective of securing against abuses. Regulation cannot therefore consist either simply in general 'norms' applicable to all citizens ('rights and duties' in the 1936 sense are a thin icing on an unpalatable cake) or in presenting the state as a unitary hierarchy of the realization of the sovereign will (that is as good as employing a watchdog with cataracts). *It is precisely because doctrines of right and sovereignty ignore the problem of the conversion of rights into capacities and the state as a realm of differentiated agencies of decision that they cannot serve to resolve the problems of socialist states.* These central categories of traditional legislation and public law are not much use. Regulation must involve mechanisms whereby administrations and administrators watch and check others (in forms that are limited): legislative and judicial specialists must have competence in problems of economic, welfare, military, etc., administration. Administrators must take part in practices of regulation, be conditioned to accept them and be interpellated by ideologies that sustain those practices. This raises the necessity of the presence on legislative bodies of the members of certain of the main agencies of decision as a condition for informed rules and their conditioning in an ideology of the necessity of preserving freedom, of administering within limits, etc. Thus enterprises, hospitals, unions, groups of specialists and so on require a presence on legislative bodies. This is not to try to resurrect Cole's *ad hoc* coordination of associations in a new form; the regulatory and control bodies in question must be specific apparatuses with capacities and a role specific to them, reaching decisions independently of the bodies they supervise and from which some of their members come. Merely to list the bodies from which personnel should be drawn as spokesmen/rapporteurs or experts (not 'representatives') would demonstrate that there could be no unitary constituency or set of 'interests'. The same mechanism of provision could not be used for these very different 'constituencies.'[6]

This role of control and supervision in so far as it is considered at all has been assigned in Marxist political theory to popular democracy. The state, while it continues to exist as a complex of specialist administrative agencies, can be checked only by a real basis of popular power. This basis is threefold: soviets/communes, factory councils, and a militia. The first point to notice here is that the category of the 'people' or 'working class' is transformed into definite organizations. The 'people' *as such* cannot act. Indeed, what the 'people' as a political entity *is* must be defined by specific organizations and by laws: its composition is the result of political decisions as to *nationality* (Marxism provides no means of determining the scope of a state territory and grounds for inclusion; socialist states are therefore forced to use criteria identical with those of bourgeois states: birth within a definite territory as with the USSR, or cultural and ethnic characteristics of persons as citizens – any ethnic Chinese can on certain conditions claim citizenship of the People's Republic, for example), age, sex and competence (madmen or former capitalists and 'bourgeois' elements may be denied political rights). The second point to notice is that, while the particular organizations of 'popular' power have *limited* administrative, supervisory and policy formation capacities, the 'people', as the creative force in socialist construction, are assigned an *unlimited* sovereignty.[7]

It is necessary to examine what these capacities are, to see what can be attained by direct democratic organization. The objective is not to deny popular democracy and self-administration any role – far from it – but to point out that it cannot perform certain tasks of administration or serve as a means of supervision of the state agencies made necessary by these very limits in its capacity.

'Direct' democracy – rule-making and administrative bodies in which every member involved in a certain activity is or can be involved – *can* be an effective means or organization under certain conditions. Units such as village communes, small factories, schools, housing estates and so on can be run in this way. It is necessary to design the scale and scope of tasks of such bodies to permit direct democracy; it is both an economical form of control and provides masses of ordinary people with an education in basic organizational skills. [8]

The limits of direct democracy arise above commune or plant level. There are three main problems. The first is the coordination of the activities and use of resources of a multiplicity of units engaged in similar activities – plants producing products needed by others, or drawing on common pools of labour, raw materials, energy, etc. Coordination of activities and distribution of resources require agencies of decision above plant/commune level. As organizations these agencies are irreducible to plant level: they are forced to make decisions affecting plants – involving clashes of line, allocations between competing uses of resources, etc. This is true even if they are composed of personnel drawn from plants through some mechanism to which a doctrine of 'representation' is attached. This level uses distinct means of administration and criteria of decision. The second problem arises from the fact that units of administration of distinct activities are not at par with one another: plants, hospitals and battalions are not of the same type. Production, medical welfare and war are distinct activities requiring different conceptions of administration and different limits of action. This means it is difficult to put the 'basic units' of any set of social relations together as the foundations of a political system:

(1)   Plants or communes, which are capable of being administered by direct democracy, cannot organize residence, welfare, etc., beyond the most basic level. The greater the 'enterprisation' of non-productive activities, the more restricted is the ability to change the form and size of the enterprise (such changes

dislocate residence, welfare funds, etc.). The provision of residence and welfare outside enterprises, e.g. a number of enterprises sharing common facilities in the form of a 'town', makes more sophisticated welfare provision and flexibility in production organization possible: otherwise the expansion, contraction and differentiation of plants poses severe problems. 'Enterprisation' also introduces severe rigidities into the labour force (plant = 'home'). It follows from this that 'towns' are aggregations too complex to be administered by direct democracy, that division of labour and specialization of activity create different interests and claims on resources. 'Factory councils' or 'communes' cannot be the exclusive basis of local organization: hospitals, schools and office councils would parallel them, while 'town councils' and means of controlling planning and allocative bodies involve elections or systems of appointment. 'Factory councils' are easily identifiable with the notion of 'workers' power' and a basic identity of interests. Social workers, nurses and doctors, economists and other specialists organized in the councils of their equally necessary agencies, and, perhaps, far outnumbering production workers, are less easily fitted to a doctrine of an homogeneous 'workers'' power.

(2) War is not a continuous activity and military units do not have autonomy to make decisions in this regard – battalion direct democracy is confined to matters of discipline and housekeeping; in other relevant matters units act on orders from higher authority.

The third problem is that direct democracy is not an 'essence' or 'spirit' that informs the higher levels of organization made necessary by its limits. The People's Republic of China illustrates this point well: extensive direct democratic institutions and practices in communes, factories, battalions, etc., are well documented, but this parallels an absence of developed institutions of control of centralized political and economic decision-making bodies, of means of discussion and criticism at regional and national level not dominated by party and state officials.[9] Direct democracy does not achieve 'popular' control over the higher levels; merely sending delegates 'upwards' to other bodies is not the answer. It assumes that recall to the base can police a series of layers of administration each of which sends delegates to the next. But no specific *means* of supervision and control of these higher bodies are proposed. Libertarians may wish for a world without nation states, extended division of labour, complex problems of economic control and allocation, the problems of urban areas, political differences and wars: let them wait for it. Under such conditions direct democracy cannot suffice as the primary means of administration and control. Marxist–Leninists stress the democratic 'dictatorship of the proletariat' over the bourgeoisie, and popular democracy is the keystone of that dictatorship. But local committees can have little impact against a single disciplined party machine and state agencies whose actions are unfettered by special-purpose bodies competent to do so. The absence of defined and enforced limits on the masses' action in conceptions of the commune state is mirrored by the actual absence of limits on the party and state apparatuses in states espousing 'Marxist–Leninist' ideologies. This conception of state stems from giving priority to the interests of transformation of social relations. In the USSR the result of this conception of state and an unfettered state machine has been the exact reverse: a block on political development. To say 'unfettered' is not to resurrect the chimera of 'absolute' power. *Any* agency is limited by the means of exercise of its activity at its disposal and the capacities of other agencies. At issue here are *limits constructed in pursuit of policy*.

It is not a matter, as we have seen, of counterposing parliamentary democracy to popular democracy. Parliamentary 'representative' democracies can also place precious few effective limits on the action of state agencies. However, the election of 'representatives' to legislative bodies by the (competent) population as a whole does have certain political advantages and can serve control functions; but its role must be assessed in terms other than its 'representativeness' (i.e. of certain prior 'interests'). There are two main advantages in such a system of voting:

(1) Certain minimum political requirements are placed on *all* (competent) agents; a legal capacity and requirements to vote interpellates all persons as political subjects. Elections serve as a means of *political education* and induction on a wider scale, just as direct democratic organization provides an introduction to administrative competence on a limited scale. The dangers of

Cole's suffrage based on *activity* are that it ignores the problems of induction to and mobilization for political activity (it treats association as a 'natural' human attribute). Elections also serve to stress the importance of the legislative and regulatory agencies. Elections can serve as an ideological focus reinforcing a generalized and mass commitment to enforcing limits on and ordered forms of the action of state and mass agencies.

(2) Elections in the USSR have served primarily as means of mobilizing expressions of 'support' for the regime. Mobilization through elections must involve such a role of reinforcement of party and certain state agencies' capacities for unregulated action if the agents, organizations and issues entering into elections are set by these very agencies. 'Pluralism' is a precondition for elections serving the functions of provision of personnel for agencies of control and development of mass political involvement and competence. Only if the means of agitation, opposition and the conduct of campaigns are widely available can different policy lines be openly debated, state and other agencies' conduct publicly reviewed, and mass commitment to enforcing regulated and ordered forms of political decision-making generated. (Conventional liberal ideologies cannot be an adequate support for this particular 'pluralism', precisely because they stress the primacy of 'representation'. A doctrine of representative democracy is not the sole answer to the problems of regulation, organization and control raised by this notion of 'pluralism'. Democratic elitist notions of 'polyarchy' are no more satisfactory; *any* state is polyarchic in the sense of involving a number of centres of decision, constituencies of support and bases for divergence of interest. The problem raised here is not of the *existence* of a plurality of differential agencies of decision, but the forms of their definition and regulation.)

I have tried to stress the central role of autonomous legislative and regulatory institutions in the control of the agencies of socialist states. The prescription of limits and practices of inspection and review cannot merely be diffused throughout social relations, as popular democratic ideologies suppose. Specific institutions claiming a *general* definitive and regulatory competence are necessary – institutions of *last resort* in questions of adjudication, that is, legislature and higher courts. I have also stressed the uselessness of the notion of 'sovereignty'. First, the legislature need have no single source of its members; its claims derive from no 'sovereign' whose will it represents but from the necessity of its functions. Second, what necessitates a complex of legislative and regulatory agencies is that the state does not take the form of a single 'sovereign' power acting according to the 'rule of law' but is a complex of agencies of decision. The delimitation of state agencies' functions and capacities cannot be based on the assumption of the state as a homogeneous public power. It is a heterogeneous domain united by definition and regulation. A legislature recruited partly by nomination, partly by indirect election from certain categories of organizations, and partly by universal suffrage conforms to no single doctrine of 'democracy'. Social organizations and administration conducted partly by direct democracy, partly by competent specialist agencies, and partly by bodies of elected and appointed 'representatives' have no unity of principle. They conform to no doctrine of democracy, whether popular or representative. 'Democracy', of whatever form, is *not an absolute value*, but a means of providing personnel to bodies that serve definite functions. Those means need have no unity.

I have contended that socialist states need a firm framework of public law and legislative regulation, precisely because socialization means that functions and capacities of state agencies increase and differentiate. It is not the *presence* of this framework that is at issue but the forms of its effectivity in defining and regulating agents' capacities. This, as we have seen, cannot be attained by merely promulgating rules; it is a matter of constructing organizations with the appropriate capacities, of practices of inspection and review, and of mass commitment to the decisions following from those practices. This cannot be attained merely by creating a legal instance; it is a question of the whole form of the socialist state and of the organized competence of its members. Equally, without certain specific definitive and regulatory institutions this whole form cannot be designed and fixed. It is a matter not of 'legality' but of the work that courts and legislative bodies do. 'Legality' can always be achieved – the USSR or Hitler's Germany make the point all too well – and it is an established prejudice of the Left to set the least possible store by it. The reason for this is that courts enforcing rules of procedure and limits to action, public discussion, opposition and organization not limited to certain favoured objectives or 'interests', and so on, are capable of serving as effective blocks to change. That these 'blocks' are a precondition for avoiding 'Stalinism', that the centralization of decision-making according to the dictates of a single popular will is a chimera, cannot be admitted except at the price of radically rethinking the character and objectives of socialist states. The orthodox Marxist Left wants to avoid 'Stalinism' but without forfeiting the political doctrines and conceptions of organizational practice that make it an ever-present danger.

PASHUKANIS AND SOCIALIST SOCIAL POLICY

Pashukanis was committed to the doctrine of the 'withering away of law', but not in the interests of libertarianism. It is the *form* of law that is to be replaced. Law works through general norms, applicable universally to individuals, and entails categories of subjectivity in its definition of fault (responsibility, intention, guilt, etc.). This corresponds in a hypostatized form to the realities of individuation in relations of commodity exchange, to individuals who make economic decisions independently of one another. Individuals can be regarded as autonomous agents whose actions depend on their will and who can be held responsible for the consequences of those actions. Linkages between individuals are primarily matters of exchange and alienation of things; regulation therefore concerns the acts of specific individuals in relation to others. In a system of collective property and planned, cooperative production, the *form* of law is inappropriate to the regulation of conduct. Individuals are not as such autonomous economic agents and must act in concert. The securing and restitution of property, the central element in both private and criminal law, is an irrelevance to the regulation of the process of production. In the transitional period of construction of a communist society, people must learn to cooperate. Traditional forms of individualism characteristic of commodity society must be eliminated in favour of socialist patterns of conduct. The notion of certain generally applicable and prescribed standards of conduct, and therefore the possibility of deviation from them, is retained. The management of this deviation for Pashukanis takes the form of 'social defence'. Law and adjudication are replaced by administrative action and political struggle (for Pashukanis's conception of 'social defence' see Sharlet, 1974). Conduct is reviewed by state agencies and one's comrades. Institutions of 'social defence' examine individuals' behaviours not in terms of fixed general rules concerning specific categories of acts, but in terms of their overall contribution to and fitness for socialist construction. Categories of intention and responsibility are not at issue; the consequences of behaviour and its forms are reviewed without reference to categories of conscious motive or fault. Instead of 'punishment', the correction or modification of behaviour is the remedy. In the place of punitive measures to coerce a calculating bourgeois subjectivity is the application of political judgement and social, psychological and medical science to the reform of conduct in the interests of socialist politics.

Pashukanis is opposed to *bourgeois* subjectivity – to the notion of the autonomous agent responsible for its acts. But he offers instead – in the implications of his programme – a new form of *subjectification*: the object of these measures is 'socialist man'. All individuals who compose the 'people' are and must be mobilized towards the attainment of this end. This mobilization takes the form of mass practice and the imposition of 'popular' standards (Comrades' Courts), but for severe or more complex cases of deviation it must also involve specialist agencies (police, psychiatrists, paediatricians, etc.). Mobilization towards socialist construction of the sort Pashukanis supports means in practice mass surveillance and the adjustment of individuals to standards considered appropriate by 'mass' and state agencies. As Foucault argues in *Discipline and Punish* (1977), there can be no system of 'discipline' – i.e. inspection of individual conduct and its adjustment to a norm – without definite forms of subjectification. 'Social defence' is in substance nothing but a system of disciplinary surveillance and behaviour modification. If Pashukanis's conception were put into operation, medical and psychiatric knowledge would be deployed by state agencies to serve the definition and enforcement of socialist 'normality'.

Pashukanis does not mention, nor did the practice of state institutions in the USSR devise, techniques of assessment and transformation of behaviour radically different from those in the 'capitalist' West. Psychiatry, paediatrics, penology and social welfare were and are derivations from the sciences and practices developed from the eighteenth century onwards by the European and American bourgeoisie. There is no distinctly 'socialist' policy or technique in matters of the medical or socially therapeutic manipulation of individuals. 'Socialist' policies, whether of reform through labour or behaviour modification, are restatements, resurrections or modifications of the programmes of 'bourgeois' reformers. The cooperative, socially pliable individual, capable of giving his full potential to the community, is no discovery of the October Revolution. Pavlov could add little to the practice of Pinel, Tuke or Rush, Makarenko nothing to Fry or Shaftesbury. The *techniques* of 'social defence' are in no sense specific to the *objectives* of a socialist society.[10]

This is no plea for Foucauldian libertarianism. It is not a plea against the inescapable oppressiveness of medical and psychiatric normalization. Medical and psychiatric intervention in compulsory forms cannot be dispensed with, except on pain of mass misery and pathology. We have no replacements for hospitals, mental homes and prisons – 'liberalizations' and 'domestications' of these institutions have been with us since *The Retreat*. *Red Bologna* (Jäggi et al, 1977), a sometime cult text of the Left on alternatives in social policy, adds little that cannot be found in UK comprehensive schools or the NHS. Foucault opposes what he considers to be a carceral 'gulag', a complex of institutions as repressive in its own way as the familiar Soviet system of camps but which in the West exists to 'discipline' deviants in the interests of social policy objectives. In line with this metaphor, he conceives law as no more than a rubber stamp that sanctions the functioning of this disciplinary system. Pashukanis proposes in 'social defence' (for the very 'best' of motives – he is no spokesman for the Stalinist police state) something that could only conform to Foucault's negative utopia of 'disciplinary society'. Both are, from opposed motives, equally misguided. Medical, psychiatric and welfare institutions and practices cannot and do not escape from, could not exist without, the forms of definition and limitation imposed by law.

Foucault's notion of a 'disciplinary society', a total system of practices of 'government' based on 'normatizing individualization', is an absurdity. These practices have no unity of objective, content or effect. Foucault can assign such unity to them only by two dubious devices: the model of the Panopticon as the essence of all disciplinary power, and the 'body' as the common referent of all disciplinary surveillance and action. Without these devices the 'strategies' Foucault amalgamates into a single force are dispersed. Foucault does *not* derive the forms of government entailed in the 'microphysics of power' or the strategies these powers embody from a prior social origin. They are not an emanation of capitalism. Nor is there a single social support behind the disciplinary 'eye', an interest or agent whose servant these powers and strategies are. They are specific constructions in discourse and entail discrete techniques and practices. The 'solutions' to problems of social organization are neither given nor homogeneous. The 'needs' of economic relations are not known outside the definite forms in which they are constructed and met. The prison is first and foremost an 'idea in architecture', a specialist enclosure of space with its own conditions of conception, construction and management. So is the factory. As a form of organization it is not privileged or automatic for being 'economic'. Such forms had to be devised, campaigned for and introduced; other forms of organization are no less possible, a definite variety of policy 'lines' always confronts the agents involved in any decision about social organization. 'Capitalism' no more made the prison or factory necessary than they sprang fully armed from the head of Mr Bentham. Foucault's *Discipline and Punish* offers us this critical lesson: it insists on the specificity of forms of 'government', and yet it destroys the value of that lesson by homogenizing the powers thus created into a single oppressive disciplinary monolith.

In *Discipline and Punish* Foucault tends to counterpose legal and disciplinary regulation. Law is conceived as limit or prohibition, whereas disciplinary power transforms and magnifies the capacities of the subjects on which it works. Law is marginalized, legal adjudication becomes secondary to a mass of normatizing interventions in the form of a knowledge of individuals through mechanisms of surveillance. But there is no opposition between law and discipline, as the author of *The Birth of the Clinic* and *I, Pierre Rivière* should know. Law defines the status of the specialist practices and sets limits to the powers of the agents and institutions involved in forms of discipline – doctors, teachers, reformatories, hospitals, etc. For example, doctors are a legally defined class of agents with an enforced monopoly over certain classes of decisions and acts. Part of their status is their capacity to assist the courts in evaluating the conditions of plaintiffs (whether insane, unfit to plead, etc.).

'Doctor' is a status in law, assigned public functions. Doctors make decisions sanctioned by law (e.g. whether an abortion is legal or not) and assist courts in making decisions. Legal regulation and the scope of legal rules lose nothing thereby. Without a publicly assigned position and legally defined exclusiveness in the performance of their role, the key institutions and agents of the 'disciplinary' region could not function: prisons, psychiatry, medicine, social work, and so on.

It is possible for Pashukanis to imagine that these agents and institutions could operate without a specific instance of regulation, without definition and review, because he considers that administration can dispense with the form of law. Law is defined by him in such a way that the role of public law is a non-issue. Specialist, medical, psychiatric, etc., interventions are necessary and will remain so, whatever the form of economic organization. At the same time it must be accepted that there are no distinctly 'socialist' standards of conduct or 'socialist' techniques of social policy that might reform their practice. If 'civil liberties' are to be secured, definite formal limits on the action of institutions such as psychiatric hospitals and social security agencies have to be imposed to prevent them from serving as means for the suppression of political opposition. In the light of these considerations, the idea that a framework of legal regulation and review be replaced by apparatuses of 'social defence' subject only to considerations of administrative objectives and effectiveness is disastrous.

The necessities of legal definition and regulation in the area of 'social policy' arise under a number of heads:

(1) The need to set standards of conduct and management for specialist institutions such as prisons, reformatories, mental hospitals, old people's homes, etc.: this involves competent agencies of regulation, inspection and disclosure independent of their immediate administrations; it also involves mechanisms whereby persons detained or undergoing treatment can obtain a review of their position according to definite formal grounds and conditions of admission.

(2) Equally necessary is the need to limit and review the powers and actions of 'mass' or communal organizations; there can be no free range for 'Comrades' Courts', cooperatives' committees, etc. Possibilities of maladministration and oppression of

minorities in factories and communes are just as real as in institutions staffed by specialists like doctors. Again, access to tribunals on the part of individuals and capacities to oversee communal institutions by review bodies are a condition of protection of opposition and difference.

(3) The conditions of monopoly of certain forms of intervention need to be carefully set so as not to exclude significant possibilities of therapy, i.e. freedom to practise for psychoanalysis, homoeopathy, acupuncture, etc., rather than a monopoly for conditioning therapy or conventional medicine (within certain limits).

(4) Involuntary commitment of individuals to therapy, the taking of children into care, etc., ought to be no less subject to judicial decision than it is in advanced capitalist countries.

'Social defence' can replace legal regulation only if *lower* standards of control of administration are accepted than pertain in the West. The same is true of any system that places reliance in matters of social policy on 'popular' democracy; mass practice has no spontaneous existence but always means definite organizations, which are no less in need of review or control than any other. Pashukanis and Foucault offer their respective visions of a regime of 'social policy' outside of law, the one a positive one, the other a negative utopia, and both are equally impossible. These views reveal in their very defects why a framework of legal regulation is essential in matters of health, welfare and reform of conduct.

In the USSR, Pashukanis's programme for the elimination of law and its replacement by 'social defence' was opposed in the name of 'proletarian law' or 'socialist legality'. These ideas have an odious parentage; no one would welcome standing on the same ground as state prosecutor Vyshinskii. The critical point of this opposition, that the state must take a definite legal form, while correct, is not at issue here. What is crucial is the nature and objectives of this legal framework. 'Socialist legality' is worthless if it means merely that there is a legal code and 'due process', and that these are at the disposal of the party and upper state echelons; by issuing orders to judicial functionaries through the Ministry of Justice *nothing* is thereby secured. The dictatorship of party leaders and state officials need not deviate one inch from strict legal rectitude (although Stalin's purges evidently did so). Unless the state machine is subject to practices of interruption, limit and control, legality and 'civil liberties' have no meaning: they are like a manufacturer's guarantee which excludes everything of value. 'Socialist legality' and 'social defence' amount to the same thing: the unimpeded centralization of state power in the proclaimed interests of social transformation. To *restore* 'socialist legality' in the USSR is to achieve precious little; the state has ample scope within the forms of law to hobble and repress its enemies. Its essays in 'illegality' are an unnecessary crudity born of long-acquired contempt for its own ineffective legal framework of control.

This contempt is no peculiarity of hardened Soviet party bosses. It is a common attitude of socialist Left and libertarian ultra-Left in the West. E. P. Thompson's impassioned appeal for socialists to accept the concept of 'rule of law' has had some effect in producing ritual acceptance of the notion that law and law enforcement are not purely oppressive expressions of ruling-class power. Thompson foolishly ascribed this wholly negative view to imaginary 'structural Marxists'. Thompson notwithstanding, far too many of the Left remain committed to the notion of socialism as the 'self-emancipation of the working class'. Socialism or communism means, as an ultimate objective, a society without complex differentiated organization, without irreconcilable differences or conflicts. I have tried to show that popular democracy cannot be the sole basis of organization, that 'mass' practice can be as oppressive as any other, and that the condition of political difference and debate of policy lines can be secured only by imposing limits on central state and mass organizations' capacities. To accept the necessity of legal regulation under socialism entails more than mouthing phrases about the 'rule of law'; it means changing the orthodox Marxist conception of the socialist state.[11]

RIGHTS AND THE SUBJECT

I have stressed the necessity for a framework of legal definition and regulation in socialist states. At the same time I have challenged the value of concepts of 'sovereignty' or 'rights' in the elaboration of this framework. This is for a number of related reasons:

(1)   Categories of 'rights' and 'sovereignty' are generally presented
      as derivations of ontological doctrines in which institutions and
      laws are conceived as the expression or recognition of certain
      prior or privileged attributes of subjects. The support of these
      attributes is a unitary and constitutive subject. The 'sovereign'
      is the people or an individual – the monarch, prince, etc.
      'Rights' are conceived as the attributes of individual human
      subjects deriving from their nature or essence, i.e. from their
      being free beings, ends rather than means, and so on. These
      doctrines, which are deployed to justify 'sovereignty' or
      'rights', always lead to a conception of social organization as
      expressive of a principle, a singular and homogeneous deriva-
      tive of the will of subjects or individuals. Such doctrines are
      incapable of sustaining the complexity and heterogeneity of
      state institutions and social relations.

(2)   It is precisely this complexity and heterogeneity that needs to be
      taken account of under 'socialization'. The defence and the
      limitation of the capacities of action of *organizations* are just as
      important an issue as those of individual subjects; this is why
      the notion of 'civil liberties' is inadequate to questions of
      effective organization, efficiency in decision-making and so
      on under socialism. To present the state as the homogeneous
      sphere of realization of a single will is to court all the dangers
      of non-recognition of its differentiation and to privilege in
      ideology certain institutions and organizations, classically the
      party and higher organs of administration. Law as regulative
      of complex differentiated agencies can best be conceived not as
      the expression of the will of a single centre, but as a means of
      maintaining and yet limiting differentiation of decision-making
      by means of certain procedures and institutions.

(3)   The capacities of public organizations are *constructed* rather than
      inherent; they have no single origin once the notion of a
      'sovereign' is challenged. Organizations have no given nature
      or attributes, and the category of 'right' fits uneasily with the
      definition of their capacities of action relative to certain specific
      objectives.

(4)   Human subjects are no more 'natural' beings with given
      attributes than organizations established in public law. The
      'rights' of individual human subjects are likewise capacities and

statuses constructed in law and convention. Subjects have no given nature of which 'rights' are the expression: the statuses and capacities of subjects are relative to the objectives of legislation and are differential (the statuses assigned to individuals are not homogeneous; viz, doctors, madmen, minors, etc.) The 'universal' statuses of civil rights establish very little; in order to be effective, they always involve the specific construction and delimitation of the powers of institutions: thus 'freedom of speech' must be specified into specific and conditional limitation of police and municipal powers, conditions of access to media, etc. All the proclaimed 'civil rights' in the world are nothing beside the organization of institutions; 'civil liberties' are a codeword for certain *effects* of the control of institutions.

Pashukanis, as we know, challenged the validity of 'right' as a category in the public sphere; for him notions like 'right of parliament' were absurd and the whole structure of public law was an ideological illusion (albeit a necessary one). This challenge to the category of right is different from mine. It arises because, on the one hand, he considered the essence of law to be *private possessive right*, the recognition of the (socio-historically given) attributes of subjects as bearers of commodities; and, on the other, he conceived the state as in reality an *unlimited* instrument of class oppression. I have argued in an earlier work (1979) that, contrary to Pashukanis, law cannot be conceived as the recognition of prior attributes and that subjects have no given form in the relations of production independent of their specific construction in law (properly, right is not a mere recognition of possession; the form of property law conditions economic relations). I have also argued that state power is limited by the means of its exercise, that these means involve the organization of the state into differentiated agencies, and that this differentiation demands definition in public law. For Pashukanis the categories of public law are derived from those of private law; law and the possessive rights of individual subjects are inseparable. Law must vanish along with the forms of real possession that generate 'bourgeois right'. Law and the category of 'right' are made coterminous.

Pashukanis's position curiously parallels that of the most sophisticated representative of modern Anglo-Saxon analytic legal philoso-

phy, Ronald Dworkin. Dworkin's *Taking Rights Seriously* (1977) is a
critical challenge to legal positivism which insists that law does not
consist in *rules* and their application alone. Legal practice must of
necessity involve reference beyond the letter of the law to 'rights'.
'Rights' are categories pertaining to the attributes of subjects that
condition the conduct of the legal process and provide means of
settling difficult disputes where questions of the interpretation,
applicability or validity of statuses arise. Legal practice constantly
generates questions about the 'fairness' of the law, whether 'justice'
will be done to individuals if a statute is rigidly applied, and so on.

   Dworkin is correct to argue that laws must involve reference to
principles and objectives that go beyond statutes. Legislation involves extra-legal considerations of the objectives served by statutes,
and practices of review by higher courts must involve principles
of judicial procedure and of application of law to cases. But there
is no reason, having said this, to argue that those objectives and
principles must always take one form – that they express the
philosophy of liberalism and involve reference to ontological
questions (the attributes of subjects). Dworkin's brilliant argument is
limited by the 'ordinary language' bias of the philosophical method
he uses. It is a form of analysis of discourse that reviews certain
bodies of statement that it selects by implicit rules of inclusion. It
examines the distribution of statements within the universe created
by such rules. It reaches conclusions about the conditionality of
certain of those statements – that they make reference to 'rights'. But
this can appear as a definitive analysis only by not questioning the
limits of the distribution of the statements in question, by not
examining the particular conditions of formulation and appearance
of statements. It is a method that has traditionally shunned the
questions re-posed in a novel form by Foucault's *Archaeology of
Knowledge*. It tells us what a particular body of legal–political
discourse and popular practices saturated by its categories tends to
produce as statements. The conditions of possibility of other
discourses of reference to the principles governing rules of law
cannot become a pertinent question. It tells us how Anglo-Saxon
lawyers and judges, within a definite range of discourses that
organize a practice of law, are constrained to speak and write. It can
tell us nothing about how the discourses organizing socialist legal
practices should be constructed. This is not to dismiss Dworkin on

his own terrain. His work is a powerful and necessary restatement of the radical tradition of classical liberalism. He is fighting a battle for 'civil liberties' against state agencies *and* for legislation to promote social justice, protect oppressed minorities, and so on. The discourse of 'rights' is a condition of argument he did not choose and cannot alter; it is a constituent element in legal and political debate in England and America. It cannot instruct us, however, in what socialist jurists should do; nor, for that matter, can it be more than a limited intervention in Anglo–Saxon legal debates. It tends to confirm rather than challenge certain of the dominant terms of those debates, *but there are others.*

I shall try to argue that reference to 'rights', to the ontological attributes of subjects, by no means provides a means of deciding 'hard cases' or questions of what interests are to prevail in legislation. It can just as well make these questions insoluble or their solution arbitrary. I shall argue:

(1) that laws can serve objectives of social policy, regulating the conduct of individuals, without interpellating subjects as bearers of possessive right; I shall take my example not from some existing or future socialist state but from contemporary England, the 1967 Abortion Act;

(2) that to the extent that categories of right and ontological reference are introduced into legislation and juridic discourse the result is to generate the claims of rival ontologies, to parallel the rights of one agent with the conflicting claims of those of another; a good example would be the Baake case, but for our purposes a more apposite example is the Paton case.[12]

The 1967 Abortion Act serves the objective of decriminalizing, under certain circumstances, abortion, thereby suspending under certain conditions the Offences against the Person Act 1861. The Act does this by assigning to doctors – a publicly defined status – the role of determining whether an abortion is legal or not. An abortion is a legal act if doctors acting in 'good faith' deem it necessary on certain specified grounds. No one speaks of doctors' 'rights' in this matter; it is one of the capacities and responsibilities as publicly recognized competent agencies assigned to them under various Acts. No subject has a 'right' to an abortion, nor is a special act of *consent* necessary.

The Act does not define any form of proprietal relation over the foetus: the father has no 'right' to consent to or withhold an abortion; a woman has no 'right' to one (indeed, in certain circumstances, abortions may be performed *without* consent); and the foetus has no 'rights' in this respect, although it is a *person* in law (e.g. under the Offences against the Person Act 1861). Mr Paton sought to claim rights in respect of the unborn child carried by his wife: he failed. Mr A. Rankin, QC, who represented him, demonstrated brilliantly that the law provided him with no grounds to act. In reviewing the law on this matter Rankin assessed the Act and was forced to question:

> whether the Abortion Act is talking about rights in the juris-prudential sense. In the Abortion Act . . . Parliament is dealing with the interests of the unborn child, in the context of eugenic permission for termination of pregnancy and the interests of the mother and the unborn child in terms of danger to her life or danger to her physical or mental health. [*Paton* v. *Paton and Trustees* BPAS, p. 21]

Further, Rankin claims, contrary to Dworkin, a radical limitation of the role of the discourse of rights in law:

> The rights with which the Courts are concerned, my lord, . . . are not after all natural or inherent rights. The law is not concerned with natural law, but they are concerned with rights, which are the construction of the law itself, and the capacity which is conferred by law. [*Paton* v. *Paton and Trustees* BPAS, p. 21]

Here we see a lawyer who, if the law permitted essentialistic arguments in this matter has every reason to use them, meticulously demonstrating that his client has no legal right or capacity to proceed in this case. He does so by reference to the powers conferred by statute, defining the subject as a person in law with a specific complex of capacities determined by statute.

Rankin opposes the categories of 'rights' and 'interests'. 'Rights' in law establish a capacity for a person to advance in the courts a claim for relief for some definite wrong or for an agent acting as legal subject for that person to make the claim. 'Interests', on the other hand, are objectives expressed in law that are secured by empowering certain personnel or agencies to make decisions, in this case for doctors to determine the validity of grounds for abortion. 'Right' is only one form by which legislation can serve objectives; it is not necessarily defined by reference to ontological attributes. 'Right' does not inhere in the subject, but is the capacity assigned to it by law. Legislation, therefore, need not necessarily create 'rights', even in the legal sense. It may secure interests by assigning tasks to personnel or agencies. It would be idle to think of this assignment as the creation of 'rights': the determination of the legality of an abortion is not a doctor's 'right', but a task he is deemed competent to perform by reason of status. Social policy objectives can be served without endowing subjects with legal 'rights' and also without grounding on ontological doctrines. This is the one great advantage of the 1967 Act – that it excludes a question of possession, of 'right' to life, etc., rigorously: it closes a space of competing claims of the legal persons involved.

'Legal' rights can be transformed by legislation. 'Right' in this sense is conditional on statute. The 'rights' Dworkin refers to exceed these conditional capacities granted by law. 'Rights' in Dworkin's full sense are part of a discourse of claims: they establish what it is the law *should* recognize. These claims are founded on ontological doctrines, that law must correspond to the nature of the subject in question. Ontological claims can be advanced from two directions – for and against the form of law. Law can be conceived as the recognition or expression of a domain of 'rights'; legislation as a process of realizing these 'rights' and making law correspond to a more or less coherent or contradictory ontological field.[13] But ontological doctrines can also challenge law; as in the form of left-wing critiques in which law is conceived as a domain of abstract 'rights', a formal expression that is forever inadequate to the conditions of the concrete realization of what 'rights' signify: freedom, equality, etc.

Both these positions are evident in the debates on the law on abortion. Left and Right seek to challenge the 1967 Act in the interests of ontological doctrines. Anti-abortionists seek to advance the 'rights' of the foetus. The foetus – as human life from the moment of conception – has a right to life and the integrity of its person. This right takes precedence over consideration of the con-venience of the mother, who must be obliged to carry the child to

birth. Certain radical feminists privatize the 'right' of the mother to
control her own body; the woman's body is 'hers' and she should
have absolute disposition over it. This argument leads to a displace-
ment of law; the 1967 Act is challenged because it makes abortion
conditional on the doctors' decisions – it is not merely a matter of the
woman's free choice. The radical feminist argument that the woman
should have unconditional control over her body, a control outside
all legal definition and limit, is coupled with or paralleled by Marxist
arguments that seek to problematize the form of law. Unconditional
abortion is a revolutionary demand capitalism cannot meet. The
1967 Act is an example of a manipulative politics of population
control in the interests of capitalist reproduction of a healthy labour
force. It seeks to control 'social problems', to prevent the social costs
of unwanted and deformed children. A woman should have an
absolute right to choose how to control her own body.

An ideal 'socialism' is the one form of society in which this
freedom can be concretized and will be a freedom outside of law.
The stigmatization of the 1967 Act as eugenic manipulation is
conditional on the notion that there will be no problems of 'social
policy' in socialist states, that they will not be faced with the regulation of health, questions of population policy, and so on. Unconditional abortion is a 'revolutionary' demand indeed; it transcends any possible form of organization of social relations. Socialist
states encounter certain necessities of regulation in the matter of
abortion in a way no different from 'capitalist' ones:

(1) Abortion requires medical intervention which becomes in-
     creasingly complicated after twelve weeks; abortion is not a
     'private' act but involves the consumption of medical re-
     sources, the provision of facilities and questions of alternative
     forms of provision. These questions of provision are not a
     matter of *a* woman's choice, but a general social question of
     health policy. Even if, as one would hope, abortion facilities are
     more fully and evenly provided, that is a matter of public policy
     and not 'private' choice.

(2) Doctors in modern capitalist *and* socialist states are legally
     defined personnel with a monopoly of certain competencies
     and who are empowered to use specialist discretion in their
     application and use. The demand for unconditional abortion,

unregulated by law, implies a de-monopolization of medical competence. This is deeply problematic. De-monopolization would mean that anyone was free to perform abortions; there would be no limit to personnel, to methods or to facilities. The possibility created by this *laissez-faire* is of a return to the era of the 'knitting needle', in the guise of alternative medicine and self-help. Even if one opposes permitting doctors to be a closed self-governing corporation, as with the GMC, and supports giving greater scope to nurses and other personnel, this means an enhancing of the legal controls over doctors and an extension of capacities to exercise skill to nurses and others. Socialist states should take the control of medical competence and the determination of means of intervention *more* and not less seriously. Compulsory preventative medicine, prohibition of smoking, and so on, imply a stronger legal framework in matters of health than we have today, whether in England or the People's Republic of China.

(3)   The notion that abortion is a matter of 'private' choice is characterized by rationalism. It denies the realities of mental illness, neuroses, distress and just plain confusion that surround our competence to perform many commonplace acts, let alone whether to have a child or not. Socialist states should, one would hope, make competent and non-coercive counselling readily available and encourage people to make use of it. They would also be confronted with regulating the severely disturbed or subnormal; mongolism, psychoses and so on will not disappear because the forms of organization of the economy have changed.

A slogan like 'a woman's right to choose' may be an effective campaigning device, especially when it means the effective provision of contraception and abortion facilities, liberalization of grounds for abortion, etc. [14] But this slogan can be operationalized only in the legal definition of capacity and the organizational provision of means. The danger of such a slogan is when it signifies an absolute and unconditional 'right' outside of law; such a demand vitiates any attainable policy objectives. The danger of the discourse of absolute 'rights' is that rights are conceived as inherent in the subject, expressions of its nature. The subject becomes a constitutive entity independent of any social relations. Take the phrase 'our right to control our bodies', frequently voiced in this connection by radical feminists. It generates the notion of the subject as inherently possessor of itself, with an absolute right of disposal over itself. The implication is that there can be no limits to bodily conduct other than those chosen by the subject itself. Limits to bodily conduct are imposed by law in the interests of social policy objectives: one is prohibited from consuming opium or driving a motorcycle without a crash helmet, and one can be compelled to enter an isolation hospital if one has an infectious disease – the list can be extended considerably. In a socialist society such limits to conduct should not be reduced and prescriptive requirements about health and bodily skill ought to be considerably increased.

The danger in the derivation of 'rights' from some ontology of a constitutive and unitary subject is that the social relations in which they are to be realized become impossible. Persons, as social subjects, are the complex and differentiated terminals of distinct capacities and requirements imposed by rules of definition of states and acquired in social practices (see Adams and Minson, 1979, for an interesting discussion of this). The subject of 'right' is an originary and unitary entity: the 'rights' deriving from its ontological attributes are *unlimited* and also *unenforceable*; definite statutes will always make rights limited and conditional. Further, a realm of absolute rights without contradiction supposes a realm of undifferentiated and equivalent subjects, but such ontologizations of 'right' are interventions in a complex field of differentiated subjects and agencies; they serve to privilege the claims of one such category of subjects. As such they are open to competing privilegings. A 'woman's right to choose' sounds unproblematic until one realizes that 'a husband's right to choose', 'a foetus's right to life', etc., can all be constructed by prioritizing different ontologies. Such categories of 'right' cannot assist in the resolution of complex questions of social policy.

The notion of a *society* that does not constrain or limit the 'will' of the subject is possible only on condition that all subjects are identical, without differentiation of attributes and will, and by making the conditions of their interaction a matter of autonomous but mutual consent. This society of constitutive subjects is most clearly formu-lated in Rousseau's *The Social Contract* (1762). It may seem a long jump from the slogans of radical feminism to Rousseau, but the conception of 'rights' as absolute, as inherent to subjects, drives one towards the conception of the subject as an autonomous possessor-of-itself and to the general will as a condition of interaction of these subjects. Taking 'rights' seriously means taking the *fabliaux* of classical liberal–democratic political philosophy seriously.

If, on the contrary, 'rights' are conceived as nothing more than the specific capacities sanctioned by laws, then the discourse of unconditional claims becomes impossible. The rights sanctioned in law need not correspond to the forms of consistency demanded by an ontological doctrine of the subject; they have no inherent unity or a single point of reference. Rather, they serve certain socially determined policy objectives and interests. The composition of legislation can reflect distinct objectives and attempts to resolve competing claims. It is correct to argue that the composition of legislation must be discussed on grounds that go beyond the existing rules of law and that competing claims must be arbitrated between or reconciled. This becomes impossible when those claims are advanced in terms of absolute rights. The category of 'right', in any sense other than capacities sanctioned by law, generates difficulties in *any* legal system, as is shown by the example of the competing claims that can be advanced in questions of abortion. The fact that it generally involves reference to a concept of subject as inherently possessor-of-itself makes it radically incompatible with the objectives of socialist ideology. Those objectives involve the extension of the legal regulation of and practices of the social formation of individual human subjects.

NOTES

1 Edward Thompson, in the conclusion to *Whigs and Hunters* (1975), defends the notion of the 'rule of law' and conceives it as embodying certain values – fairness, equity, etc. These values are, however, problematic: law follows from certain procedural rules. The ideology of 'rule of law' is double-edged; it unifies *all* laws as equal parts of that rule. Every statute, every bit of judges' bodging to cover 'gaps' in the law, is valid and binding – the Industrial Relations Act 1971 as well as the laws proscribing acts that are universally condemned, like murder and rape. No wonder it is so popular with characters like Paul Johnson or Lord Hailsham.

2   This may seem a harsh judgement on two of the most original thinkers on questions of socialist organization, and two leaders most willing to recognize the specifity of organizational questions and the means to tackle them. However, neither Mao nor Lenin could break from the conception of a single-party state or the need to assign powers of strategic decision to the centre. In both cases the notion of a unitary 'working class' or 'popular' interest capable of expression in a single centre vitiated their own specific innovations. Lenin's last texts took an immense step back from the Bolshevik 'forced march' conceptions of socialist construction, but his organizational solution – the Workers' and Peasants' Inspection, for example – responds to the problems of control of party and state by further emphasizing the intrinsic value of the *social origin* of the personnel. Regrettably, his token 'toilers' could have been no match for skilled party and state functionaries. The solution to the problem was thought in terms of the 'proletarianiza-tion' of party and state. This was nothing but a disaster. Actually, many of the higher state administrative bodies and official function-aries – Rykov, Tomsky, Frumkin, Gosplan, etc. – were more capable of managing affairs and devising a viable strategy for socialist construction than either the party rank and file or the various 'Lefts' (including Stalin after 1928). 'Stalinism' was, among other things, a *coup d'état against* competent state administration, and socialist special-ists were its chief victims.

3   Lenin's *State and Revolution* (1917) obliterates the analysis of the specificity of the political he derived from Kautsky and further developed in *What is to be Done?* (1902). I am not simply endorsing Kautsky. Kautsky did not abandon class essentialism; he continued to conceive socialism as a necessary consequence of capitalist class antagonisms, but he did radically qualify the political conditions of its expression.

4   For Cole, the condition of association and of the interrelation of associations was fellowship; he assumes an essential harmony on the basis of which associations act. A systematic legislative government was not necessary; coordination problems could be resolved by a 'constitutional judiciary' (Cole, 1921, p. 137), but one free to make *ad hoc* decisions.

5   The promulgation of the 1936 Constitution at the beginning of the terror was a gross and vulgar joke played by Stalin on the Soviet citizenry and the able and honest men who helped to draft it – Bukharin and Pashukanis among others. But the excesses of a Stalin cannot hide the worm in the bud. Bukharin and Pashukanis were almost as far from conceding the need for checks in the capacities of

central state agencies, for a radical differentiation of the functions of state agencies, and for the necessity of erecting effective means to review and proscribe, if necessary, policies and actions.

6 The same considerations apply to courts as bodies of review, supervision and definition of limits. Adjudication and legislation are not separate; courts can be both makers and arbiters of rules. A condition for effective courts is that judges and lawyers are not officials of or under a ministry of justice, receiving orders from higher echelons of the administration and using their judgement only within limits established for them in advance. Specialist jurists are necessary, but the danger of a corps of judges is evident. Non-specialist members of courts, elected or called at random, election of judges, etc., are mechanisms to supplement juridic competence with considerations of wider interests and prevent the formation of a closed corporation of specialists.

7 The fact that there is no distinctly *socialist* conception of nationality, age of majority, conditions of socio–political competence, etc., is not a point of criticism of the practice of socialist states. Only those who believe socialism is a society-totality conferring its distinctive features on every aspect of life will be disturbed by the absence of distinctly 'socialist' positions on social policy questions. Socialist states may differ in these matters, and it is an open question of debate whether different solutions to social policy problems are better or worse. The fact that certain solutions resemble those of 'capitalist' states cannot in itself be sufficient grounds for criticism.

8 The slogan of abolishing the division of 'mental and manual' labour goes hand-in-hand with a conception of social organization as the couple to popular democracy and the centralized expression of common 'interests'. This slogan is inadequate because specific organizational forms and competencies cannot be dispensed with if complex activities are to be administered *and* the consequences of authoritarian centralization challenged. Basic administrative skills are a condition for broad political involvement, and for an informed and politically competent populace. But they are merely a starting point. Specialist skills of administration and organization – economic management, engineering, medicine, etc. – are also necessary; these must differentiate the population into distinct occupational competences that are not at par with one another. Likewise, decision-making must be performed by and be accountable to definite specialist bodies, not the 'people' as a whole. This is not a problem if forums for the debate of the decision on policy issues, forms of limitation and interdiction of action, and means of inspection and review are de-

veloped appropriate to the control of the differentiated agencies of decision.

In an earlier work, *Social Evolution and Sociological Categories* (1976), I argued strongly for popular democratic forms of administration and for the generalization of competencies among the populace. I am no less committed to these objectives now. What that earlier work chooses to ignore – as so many leftist texts do – is the problems of administering a complex state and economy solely by these means. It is these problems I have tried to examine here.

9   Chen Erjin (1984) is a most interesting discussion by a Marxist militant and worker of the Chinese state and its defects. It is a striking criticism of the Cultural Revolution from the standpoint of socialist construction. Direct democracy cannot possibly control a system in which there is a single dominant political party with tentacles and loyal members in every walk of life and when that party also controls a hierarchically organized state. Erjin calls this 'unicorporate publi-social production'; this is a concept that, like its Western equivalent 'totalitarianism', greatly overestimates the unity, the power of control and the coherence of action of the socialist state. Erjin's solution is a curious marriage of Mao Tse-tung and Thomas Jefferson, in which two rival communist parties, government and opposition, periodically present themselves for election. This may appear far-fetched, but it testifies to the prestige of Western representative democracy in state socialist countries where its elementary benefits are lacking and its faults are dwarfed by the defects of the prevailing regimes. It also makes the point that political pluralism, in the sense of the relatively open competition of political forces, is a precondition for any kind of free public life. Erjin, however, proposes only a manacled pluralism – whether for reasons of his own safety or not I do not know – in which the competitors swear to construct socialism. Despite his enthusiasm for representative democracy and the separation of powers, Erjin, not surprisingly, fails to see how compatible they are with a powerful centralized state system, even in the USA. He still conceives the state as a single dominant public power. He has (not surprisingly) no knowledge of that current of 'pluralism' in Western political theory that challenges that concept of the state and seeks to promote a number of levels and dimensions of authority, each with its own autonomous existence that is not a mere concession of the central state.

10 Communitarian and populist practices of control and adaptation, such as were introduced in China during the Cultural Revolution, are not the same as 'social defence'. The latter notion involves the intervention

of specialist knowledgcs and state agencies. But the popularization of normatization and control is not an unproblematic alternative to 'social defence'. Mass practice unlimited by general rules of conduct relating to specific classes of act can be no less oppressive than norms of conduct enforced by medical or psychiatric functionaries.

11 In the original (1980) version the above paragraph included some remarks sharply critical of Jock Young and others. It would be fatuous to let old differences remain frozen when the circumstances they related to have long disappeared. Jock Young is now foremost among those trying to beat some sense into the Left about law and order, whilst not neglecting to criticize the very real defects of policing methods and the administration of justice – see Lea and Young (1984).

The discussion of law and socialism has also improved considerably since the first version of this chapter was published. Bob Fine (1984) clearly recognizes the need for Marxists to avoid the outright rejection of liberal democracy as 'bourgeois domination'. He clearly recognizes the need to struggle for civil liberties and for democratic controls on public authority. Where he ultimately falls short of the radical rethinking necessary for socialists is in his conception of socialism, which remains obstinately marooned in the nineteenth century. This stateless utopia, in which formal democracy and the rule of law become superfluous because politics and law as such have 'withered away', condemns all struggle for attainable reforms and institutions to be a mere makeshift in the course of a long struggle for the final supersession of bourgeois right. Tim O'Hagan (1984) certainly does not suffer from this defect. O'Hagan argues why socialism can only be a complex and pluralistic society based on mass administration and modern industry, and, therefore, must be an 'open *gesellschaftlich* society'. O'Hagan counterposes a *Rechtsstaat*, an advanced liberal society, as a desirable social and political ideal to the impractical but dangerous rhetoric of a communal society without formal political structures.

12 I am grateful to Parveen Adams for originally drawing my attention to the importance of the Paton case and to the full transcript of the legal argument.

13 Dworkin accepts fully that rights and claims are not coherent; that rights conflict and must be reconciled or arbitrated by the law itself. His position is subtle and complex, no mere restatement of natural law doctrines. At the same time he conceives certain 'rights' as having priority, even against statute. In the end this conception can be secured only by a doctrine of primacy, by privileging certain entities and attributes.

14 In the present situation, positive proposals on abortion law reform must necessarily be rather speculative. The key issue confronting pro-abortion campaigners is to defend the 1967 Act and minimize the damage done by Tory 'reform'. However, in the long run the only possible means of increasing abortion facilities is to push for positive legislation on the one hand and the NHS reorganization on the other. The objective of positive legislation should be to circumscribe doctors' discretion in the matter (although it would be difficult to abolish it without eliminating doctors' medical and psychological judgement) and to extend competence in determining the legality of abortion to other agents (day centre nurses and so on). The objective of legislation on NHS reorganization would be to compel the Secretary of State to provide certain facilities in each area. Even so, given professional resistance, doctors' and nurses' claims for freedom of conscience provisions, and administrative tardiness, the results of such action might be far from satisfactory. One effective short-term remedy to such deficiencies would be to strengthen the legal position of the charities (BPAS, PAS, etc.). Licensed charities could then be recognized as agencies competent to determine the legality of abortion and the DHSS required to reimburse their charges for residents of the UK who qualify for NHS treatment. Although this means formally strengthening 'private' medicine it is probably the most effective way round the resistance of Catholic doctors and the DHSS bureaucracy.

3 *Socialist Legality*

Tom Campbell's *The Left and Rights* (1983) is a conceptual analysis of the place of the categories of rights and legal rules in socialist society. Campbell is concerned to question the views of many socialists who reject the appropriateness of these categories to socialist social systems. They do so, according to him, on a number of grounds:

(1)   that rights are intrinsically tied to a competitive capitalist society in which supposedly autonomous individuals pursue self-interested claims against one another, whereas in a properly socialist society individuals will be cooperative and altruistic and not divided one from another by the self-interests of the capitalist market and by a system of production based on private property;

(2)   that rights and legal rules entail a legal formalism that is at odds with the substantive goals of socialism and can only serve as barriers to their attainment;

(3)   that competing rights, claims and formal legal rules are tied to a coercive state system, whereas under socialism the repressive apparatus of the state and the need for external controls on individuals' conduct through sanctions will disappear;

(4)   that the discourse of rights is a moralizing discourse inappropriate to the realism of socialist political practice and the attainment of its political objectives; it ties socialist political thought and language to the very illusions of liberal individualism that socialism criticizes and seeks to supersede.

Campbell claims that these criticisms are mistaken, that there is a place for rights and legal rules in socialist societies and these categories need not be tied to the bourgeois individualistic view of man and society. The benefit of socialists retaining such categories is that they provide a clearer way of relating and comparing liberal individualist and socialist claims about society, fostered by a language that uses common categories. Liberals and socialists can therefore talk to one another and rationally comprehend their differences, something that cannot happen if their views of society are held to be absolutely distinct and incompatible. Campbell says:

> If the ideals of socialism can be expressed in terms of individual rights then, however different socialist rights may be from those most highly prized by the classical liberals, there is at least a continuity and similarity of thought forms and basic concepts in which major political disagreements can be clarified and debated. [1983, p. 1]

The virtue of such an enterprise is very much taken for granted in that it supposes common terms are the basis for a rational dialogue between men of different opinions but of a common good will. This can be disputed on two grounds. First, the possession of a common language does not necessarily further either the will to agree or moderation in debate. Christian theologians, for example, have long possessed a common language with terms such as 'God', 'Salvation', 'Redemption', etc., but this has never prevented ferocious doctrinal differences and schisms, nor has it promoted clarity about differences. The modern ecumenical dialogue is not the result of Christians possessing common means of discourse; the different churches and sects still have ample sources for doctrinal difference, as the reactionaries in the various congregations are at pains to point out. It is the common social marginalization of their religious practices that drives the Christian churches to seek agreement in making a better common front against secularization and materialist ideologies. Likewise communists, socialists and liberal democrats could ally in the Popular Front, despite incompatibly expressed ideologies, because of the common threat of fascism. People can agree in the absence of a common theoretical language and violently disagree even when they possess one.

Second, the most pressing contemporary issues are hardly furthered in their resolution by agreement between liberal and socialist political philosophers about their respective social 'ideals', since these urgent problems have overtaken the nineteenth-century aspirations and assumptions on which both are based. Agreement as to terms is likely to be an agreement to cosily ignore the future. Peace and war? We face the threat of socialist and capitalist societies divided into ever more menacingly armed camps. A viable inter-national order will not be furthered by socialists claiming that the Eastern bloc does not represent their ideal of a socialist society or by well-meaning liberals claiming (against all evidence) that their creed is ultimately pacificistic. Ecological crisis? Both positions have beeen wedded to belief in the virtues of natural science harnessed to economic growth and material progress. Economic reform, East and West? Neither cause is helped by 'ideals' but by facing the flawed realities of both systems and accepting that the high-minded claims made for both by their respective ideological champions are an obstacle to doing so. Dialogue can help only if liberals and socialists perceive their own and each others' errors, and it also needs to be based on new thinking that is at once less utopian and also less exclusively committed to a single social programme. Being clear about our old ideals and aspirations is all very well but it hardly helps to get over the mutual and long-established deficiencies of classical liberalism and revolutionary socialism. We need to think in new ways about new problems rather than seek to promote dialogue between old and evidently unsatisfactory 'ideals'.

It should be evident that my criticisms of Campbell are not directed toward arguing that socialist societies can dispense with a legal order or legal regulation. In Chapter 2 it was argued that socialist states do need a clear framework of public law. Such a legal order cannot be understood either as an actualization of the claims of Marxist revolutionary socialism or as an importation of liberal pluralism, but rather must be seen as a complex of specific insti-tutions conforming to no pre-given ideological plan.

One's unease about Campbell's concern to promote dialogue is furthered rather than removed by his strategy for persuading socialists to 'take rights seriously'. He says that 'if we are to make progress with the conceptual tasks before us . . . to say whether rights are compatible with socialism' will depend 'on what counts as socialism' (p. 8). He eschews the task of defining 'genuine' socialism or of facing the fact that what is infelicitously called 'actually existing socialism' is all we are ever likely to get. The socialists Campbell seeks to engage in dialogue clearly do not regard existing socialist states with any favour or as even the most tarnished approximations to their 'ideal'.

Campbell's strategy is as follows:

> Fortunately, this problem can be circumvented to some extent by adopting the permissive line of granting the socialist critics of rights almost all that they desire by accepting, for the sake of argument, their particular versions of what a socialist society would be like. This means, in the main, accepting a relatively extreme form of socialism according to which it involves the belief in the possibility and desirability of the successful pursuit of a society characterised by the self-conscious deployment of all human and natural resources . . . to satisfy the needs of 'social' man, whose behaviour will be marked by unsullied sociability, developed social responsibility, willing cooperation, and the virtual absence of aggression, hostility, competitiveness and the desire to dominate others. [p. 9]

He concludes:

> If it can be established that even in such an ideal society there would still be occasion to maintain and protect individual rights, then the revolutionary critique of the significance of rights will have been adequately answered. [*ibid.*]

The problem is that Campbell's thought experiment involves a curious *non sequitur*. Grant all that the believers in 'true' socialism require and this proves the relevance of rights categories to socialist discourse in general. If it does not, as indeed is the case, then one would be forced to argue how realistic or sensible such an 'ideal' society is, and this Campbell does not do. Actually positing such an 'ideal' society makes it *easy* to assume the existence of individual rights that are compatible with socialism and the possibility of a non-coercive legal order. Just as easy as positing man in a state of nature driven by naked self-interest makes it possible to justify a social compact establishing the coercive regulation of conduct and the political protection of the self-interested rights claims of each in so far as they are compatible with those of others. Hobbes' conception of human nature and political society is of precious little use in considering modern capitalist societies or their legal systems, since modern capitalism is the actualization of *no* variant of classical liberal political philosophy. The same can be said of the vision of an 'ideal' socialist society. Competitive individualism and cooperative altruism alike offer generalized solutions to a 'problem of order'. They do so by supposing a social system peopled by representative individuals compatible with its basic characteristics: in the one, persons who submit to rules because of considerations of self-interest when faced with sanctions; in the other, persons who accept rules as rational guides in their cooperative interaction and therefore require no sanctions in order to obey them. Both assumptions are implausible, because of the very device of a social system explicable in terms of the generic motivations of the typical subjects who people it.

Campbell's conceding a social order in which certain generic individual attributes and motivations are assumed enables him to reduce questions of social organization to accomplished fact. Coercion can be dispensed with because of the attributes of the socialist individual. Social rules will remain necessary to determine individuals' role capacities and entitlements. These rules are best thought of as a legal system and can be done so without difficulty since coercion is no necessary part of the concept of law. Such rules confer 'rights' in the sense of capacities established in positive law or claims that such capacities ought to be conferred. Campbell's ability to establish the compatibility of a legal order with such an 'ideal' socialist society hinges on his accepting the claims of its proponents that it will lead to a certain typical personality. On this basis he can show that law, shorn of its unacceptable features, no longer gives rise to the anxieties socialist critics have about it. Indeed, but so what? In no sense does it follow that because law and rights can be made compatible with a certain discourse about an 'ideal' socialist society this has any relevance to a wider range of socialist discourses about other circumstances. If we do not accept this 'ideal' as an attainable actuality then very real problems arise about the place of law in socialist societies, especially with regard to sanctions and coercion. Campbell has made it all too easy for a certain type of revolutionary socialist ideologue to accept the categories of law and rights. He has done so by accepting premises that render such categories harmless to such an ideology. The problem is to face the fact that law in a much less sanitized sense may be necessary for those socialist systems that are attainable, to confront revolutionary illusions head on rather than to concede to them in advance.

THE MORALISM OF RIGHTS

In defining the category of 'rights' that is to be made acceptable to socialists Campbell is forced to argue against the claim that to talk of 'rights' is to engage in vacuous moralizing incompatible with the struggle for socialism or the objectives of a socialist society. He does so by rejecting the relevance to law of the category of 'moral rights' and by insisting on a positivistic account of rights as legal rights. Campbell says:

> Unless, therefore, it is being argued that there is a 'moral law' analogous to positive law to which we must make reference to find out the proper content of positive law (the natural law tradition) it is better to drop the misleading terminology of 'moral rights' or to use it only to refer to those rights which the speaker believes ought to exist, and thus make it easier to bring into the open the fact that actual positive rights may be justified by the whole range of moral values. [p. 19]

This is fair enough but, as we shall see, Campbell's conception of socialist legality, as those rules governing the conduct of a (socialist) rational being that are worthy of uncoerced obedience as such and generalizable as a norm of conduct for all such beings, comes perilously close to a Kantian conception of a moral law. Campbell, however, does not treat rights merely as positive rules endowing individuals with capacities or as claims that such rules should exist. Indeed, as Ronald Dworkin points out, to 'take rights seriously' involves reference beyond rules to principles. Such principles must come into action when rules clash or where there is ambiguity about a rule, that is, in 'hard cases'. Rights, if they mean something more than merely the bundle of capacities that existing laws happen to confer on individuals, must involve reference to an ontological dimension.

Campbell argues against my view expressed in Chapter 2 that the recourse to 'rights' discourse leads to incompatible claims to priority by competing interests, and that those claims therefore have to be resolved in terms other than rights. In that Chapter, I argued against Dworkin that to invoke 'rights', even when defined in terms of principles, cannot in fact solve hard cases. Rather, in the hardest of cases, competing rights claims based on divergent interests have to be resolved by other methods if one of them does not have clear priority under a rule. In such cases the courts must refer to the respective merits of the interests involved and may well bring public policy considerations into the decision. The ontological claims that competing interests make for their rights claims will not assist the making of a decision since these will be legally undecidable and probably morally on a par.

Campbell challenges my view not so much by disputing it as by evading it. He says:

> Such objections are apposite to moral rights whose ontological status as non-observable possessions or attributes of individuals is indeed problematic as is reflected in the insoluble conflicts which arise over what rights people actually have. But the same objection does not apply to positive rights . . . which are determinable social phenomena whose existence can be ascertained with some objectivity. [p. 24]

Which is to ignore hard cases and, one presumes, to suppose that positive law will not generate such. If Campbell means that we can find out what capacities are conferred on individuals by legal rules then he is clearly right. Rights in this sense are *legal rights*, and Chapter 2 makes clear that rights in this sense are not problematic – to the degree that they are dogmatic and relatively unambiguous (dogmatic in the sense that principles and moral categories do not enter in the domain of legal rules in question, and unambiguous in that such rules-conferred capacities are not systematically incompatible with others). But the presence of 'rights' discourse in law and legal practice is also a determinable social phenomenon that can be objectively ascertained, as has been done by Dworkin. Campbell seeks to make 'rights' a descriptive rather than an evaluative term, 'albeit descriptive of social norms' (p. 26). But legal systems do not typically consist only of unambiguous norms: for example, the American courts, as Dworkin shows, are prey to moral argument even when deciding whether a case falls under a rule, and legal rules sometimes do invoke ontological justifications for the capacities they sanction, as in the French doctrine of intellectual property analysed by Bernard Edelman (1979). Campbell's case amounts to saying that legal positivism eschews natural rights or other moralizing about rules and so socialists, if they are positivist enough, need not be upset about calling the capacities conferred by the established rules in their ideal socialist society 'rights'.

If anything, I was open to be considered as naive as Campbell in my earlier view, appearing to suppose that rights discourse in a non-descriptive and moralizing sense was an eradicable blemish in legal systems. My colleague Alan Hunt (1982) thus charges me with positivism and argues that as rights claims continue to be pressed against positive law so socialists can and should legitimately use rights discourse. Indeed, Hunt is correct to say that the construction of claims and the pursuit of legal reforms in rights terms will not go away, but that is merely to demonstrate the chronic ineradicability of a problematic practice. For Hunt does *not* show that the use of rights discourse helps to resolve hard cases or that clashes between claimed rights do not have to be resolved in terms of constructions in non-rights forms of the relative merits of the interests in question. We have both to take the continued existence in legal systems of rights discourse in the moralistic sense seriously, as something we cannot write out of the legal sphere, *and* accept that such discourse does not generally help in solving problems. I would therefore stick to the claim that invoking rights categories is no solution to the legal problems of socialist societies, in particular the issue of civil liberties. The issue here is not the use of rights categories but defensible and enforceable legal capacities of citizens that are not hopelessly ambiguous or readily evadable by state agencies.

Campbell is in fact forced to introduce ontological considerations into the analysis of rights when arguing that rights categories need not be inherently tied to competitive individualism. In order to do this he introduces an interest theory of rights, in the sense that 'ascribe a right to X presupposes that the right bearer is either interested in X, or something to which X is causally or instrument- ally related' (p. 98). Individuals may have interests 'in' things other than purely selfish goals; interest rights in a socialist society would thus include those capacities and resources whereby an individual can contribute to cooperative projects and the welfare of others. This sounds admirable. But the construction of a right to X as being something an individual is interested in or is capable of being interested in involves the supposition that the bearer of the right is capable of knowing and recognizing that X. Campbell says:

> The requirement that right bearers satisfy the condition of conative consciousness is broad enough to encompass nearly all human beings who are biologically alive and gives some sort of guideline to apply to such borderline cases as animals (the 'higher' animals clearly being included as potential right-bearers), human 'vegetables' (who may be defined as lacking consciousness and therefore as not having rights) and human foeti at various stages of development. Thus we would have some basis for saying that foeti at the early stages of development can have no rights, and that whether or not they do so at later stages will depend on empirical assumptions about the emergence of consciousness. [pp. 99–100]

Ontology enters into this argument because Campbell's position makes it necessary to ask, what kind of being can support a right? To define rights in terms of 'interested in X' presupposes being *able* to take an interest in X; it is this ability that establishes a legitimate relationship between an individual and a right. Foetuses and persons on life support machines therefore lack rights. Corporations are merely legal fictions for the interests of individuals – they 'cannot be literally concerned about anything since they lack consciousness and desires' (p. 98). Such fictions are tolerable because 'they have to do with the concerns of sentient beings' (*ibid*).

This ontological doctrine can be questioned on both positive and moral grounds. The foetus on conception is a person in law and may not be injured except in special legally sanctioned circumstances. In positive terms the foetus has a 'right' to life in that it may not be unlawfully killed and that to do so is a criminal offence. The foetus cannot pursue that right on its own behalf any more than a murdered adult can, but it does have legal rights under the 1861 Offences against the Person Act. Persons on life support machines are an area of current debate and concern, but Campbell's position simply eliminates the genuine legal and moral points of dispute and simply asserts that they have no rights. Company law in the UK treats the corporate body as a legal person in its own right: its property is distinct from that of its subscribing shareholders and it is held to have interests and purposes of its own, distinct from those of its directors and shareholders. Since Salomon v. Salomon & Co. it has been clear that the 'sentient beings' who manage it may be held at fault if they do not give due regard to these distinct interests. UK law thus does not treat the company as reducible to the sum total of the wishes or the interests of its shareholders, directors or managers. The law is committed to no ontological suppositions about corporate personality, whether of an organicist or methodological individualist kind; it merely recognizes or creates certain entities and ascribes rights to them.

Morally Campbell's doctrine is also open to dispute. It supposes consciousness as the ground for rights claims. Dogs may or may not have rights but people on a life support machine do not. Dogs may have rights but presumably fish do not. Adult 'conscious' humans are the typical bearers of rights; other entities are 'borderline' cases. Campbell apparently supposes consciousness to be an 'empirical' matter, but it is an inescapably philosophical category, not a property of beings like height or weight or the presence or absence of a central nervous system. If one were mischievous one might suggest that persons who are asleep have no rights, and so on. To construct the basis for rights in this manner is precisely to generate the sort of undecidable 'borderline' cases we cannot avoid once we insist that a right flows from an essential attribute. Campbell is not a consistent positivist or he would have to say that rights are what the laws confer, and if the attributes of the beings in question form no single class then so be it.

Campbell may say that he is here concerned with *justifications* of rights rather than positive rights themselves. But this hardly helps him in the moral domain and it leads to incoherence in the positive – the existence of legal persons who 'ought' not to have rights if the doctrine justifying rights is taken seriously and is to have any bearing on the content of law. If it does not have such bearing, its role as a justification is unclear.

Rather than taking rights to be concerned with those things conscious human beings are interested *in*, it is better to consider rights as legal protections of the interests *of* entities whose attributes may be various. In this sense foetuses, human vegetables, and so on, may be said to have interests attributed to them that the law ought to secure or to be of interest and concern as a matter of public policy and legal protection exercised on their behalf. Interests in this sense may give rise to rights in the form of legally sanctioned capacities, even if they are represented by others as active parties in law. Rather than look for some attribute as an entitlement to a right, we should accept that the beings we seek to protect in law may well be diverse; in some cases it will make sense to refer to that protection as giving them rights, in others it may not.

LAW AND COERCION

Campbell argues that even in an 'ideal' socialist society there would be social norms and more or less elaborate sets of rules. These would be necessary both for social control and for the organization of complex activities. Indeed, such systems of rules would include 'authority conferring rules' (p. 50) necessary to delimit access to posts necessary for coordination and direction. This is all very well and good, and presumably makes sense to anyone who does not equate socialism with the purely spontaneous self-activity of individuals.

Campbell goes on to argue that such a system of rules will be a legal system in part. It will involve a set of rules of recognition whereby social rules are confirmed as authoritative and legitimate and also courts to settle disputes and pronounce on rule infractions. But it will not be coercive and will not involve a state with its repressive apparatus.

Campbell argues that coercion is external to the concept of law and so it appears is the state. Challenging the very different theories of Hans Kelsen (1945, 1967) and H. L. A. Hart (1961), he contends that coercion's association with law rests merely upon certain questionable assumptions about human nature. He says: 'Hart assumes, because of certain "truisms" about human nature, that some violations of valid laws are inevitable and argues that if these violations are not met by sanctions then the benefits of law will be lost' (p. 76). Against Kelsen he argues that coercion is no necessary part of a 'pure' theory of law and that Kelsen has confused general philosophical postulates with merely local sociological generalizations about conduct and its control in particular types of society. He concludes: 'Whether or not law is coercive can thus be seen as essentially a sociological dispute concerning the possibility of a non-coercive society' (*ibid*). We can therefore relegate 'coercion to the status of a purely contingent extra-legal support for legal systems' (p. 78).

Campbell argues that Hart accepts that a legal system exists only if it is generally obeyed in the area it claims to cover and that most persons follow legal rules because they accept their legitimacy and the obligation to do so. Law for Hart is not therefore merely a set of commands of the sovereign backed by force. He goes on to say:

> Once it is allowed that some individuals obey laws because they regard legal duties as a species of moral obligation (the obligation being to obey those rules which are regarded as non-optional according to recognised procedures), then there is no reason why this should not hold for all individuals. And even if conformity to law is not universal in a society, it is not at all clear that, were a small number of deliberate violations of these rules to be marked by no more than social criticism, this would mean that the system of rules loses its legal character. [p. 78]

Socialism will produce the 'revolution in human motivation' (p. 146) that makes just such an uncoerced obedience to rules recognized as legitimately possible. But this revolution will not remove the need for adjudication:

> while it might well be the case that the sharp divide between the stigma arising from an adverse criminal decision and the more socially neutral consequences of civil proceedings would evaporate, the elimination of sanctions would not necessarily remove the guiding, educative and even denunciatory functions at present fulfilled by the criminal law. . . . Some rules infractions will always require to be identified, proved and pronounced upon, so that criminal law of a non-punitive sort would be retained as one area in which the language of rights and obligations would have a prominent function. [p. 147]

Campbell rests his argument against coerciveness on a 'sociological' presupposition, just as much as he supposes Kelsen and Hart to do – that a socialist society will produce cooperative, altruistic and non-violent persons who obey rules because they are rational and perceive them to be legitimate. Do we need to make either supposition about human nature? A social order leading to necessary consequences can be constructed supposing beings of the most diverse types, on one condition – that their attributes are in conformity with its basic principles of organization. Kant, for example, says: 'The problem of organising a state . . . can be solved even for a race of devils, if only they are intelligent' (*Perpetual Peace*, p. 112). But can and should we make such suppositions about the general attributes of social agents such that they conform to the basic principles of organization of the systems they inhabit? Is it not more apposite to make no such providential suppositions, even if the providence in question does no more than guarantee that evil persons are intelligent enough to fear sanctions. If we start from the proposition that persons are not mere artefacts of culture and that in consequence human motivations are diverse, we reach the conclusion that some persons will obey rules because of internalized conceptions of obligation most of the time and that some others will not some of the time. Hart's 'truism' can be reformulated in this manner without falling into the trap of postulating a 'human nature' that is generically and typically selfish. In which case we can say that sanctions rest not on unfortunate certainties about human motivation but on unavoidable uncertainties about the conduct of human agents and their rationales for such conduct.

Further, Campbell tends to equate sanctions and coercion, in the sense that coercion is a technology for modifying individuals' behaviours by means of force. This equation is problematic for a number of reasons. Emile Durkheim points out that even in a 'society of saints' there will be rules and infractions of those rules. Campbell would doubtless accept this, for even in his 'ideal' socialist system courts will pronounce on conduct in order to exercise 'guiding, educative and denunciatory functions'. He sees these functions as being exercised in a 'non-punitive' manner. But this is to elide punitiveness, coercion and sanction: only if the three are substantially the same can he argue that the absence of punitive means implies the absence of coercion and sanctions. Definite means of 'punishment' are not sanctions but the means used *to* sanction. Such means signify sanctions but they may well not have the effect of being *punitive*, that is, they may well not work in 'punishing' subjects, such that they feel either pain or loss, or modify conduct. Sanction as such is not extrinsic to the concept of law and in any given legal system the means of punishment that stand for sanction are legally regulated.

It is not the case that means of punishment are some administrative convenience or technology external to law, since legal systems prescribe and regulate the methods used to stand for sanction. There is, however, no intrinsic relation between sanction and any of the definite means by which it has been represented. The category of sanction is, however, *intrinsic* to law in that what differentiates a legal system is the *claim* to be the dominant and obligatory mode of regulating conduct in a definite domain. Dominance and obligatoriness are not considered to be matters of voluntary compliance or even to have the moral force of an 'ought'; they have the compelling and non-moral status of a 'must'. How or whether such compulsion is effected is another matter.

Social criticism and denunciation may well serve as means to sanction and may be no more or less effective than the most gross and violent physical punishments. We need make no assumptions about motivation here. The sword and the gallows have worked no better with unregenerate humanity than do probation or attendance centres. The question of whether or not punishments 'work' is a secondary one (and we know that to a significant degree they do not). This is beside the point: both the mildest and the most violent punishments (however effective) *signify* sanctions, but sanction cannot be identified with punitiveness. It appears that Kelsen is thus less at fault in specifying law as a sanction-stipulating norm if we are clear that sanction, coercion and particular forms of punishment mean different things. Obligatoriness implies compulsion in the sense of 'must' but it does not specify *how* compulsion is to be effected. If Campbell says that coercion is to be understood by our sense of 'must' – a rule imposed externally on individuals – then the laws acceptable to him as properly non-coercive have no more force as rules than 'ought' or 'should' and as such are not different from moral rules.

Campbell says:

If there were a system of rules, both primary and secondary, applying to and generally followed in a given geographical area and involving the standard legislative and judicial agencies with the exception of a police force and prison service with the authority to use force, then it is far less misleading to speak of a no doubt untypical legal system than a system of social norms'. [p. 79]

Law, therefore, consists in a set of primary rules that function as guides to action and a set of rules of recognition whereby actors can verify the validity of rules. Obedience is a function of the internalized acceptance of legitimacy. But how is law here differentiated from other classes of rule except by the presence of rules of recognition? Indeed, do not company rules, school rules, etc., also involve rules of recognition? Does this make them laws or a legal system? Can we differentiate laws by reason of their properties as classes of rule? The answer surely is that laws are differentiated as classes of rule not by any formal properties but by the claim advanced by the agencies issuing them to be the dominant and obligatory source of binding rules in a given territory. They take precedence over all other rules and the agencies issuing them insist on the capacity to regulate all other rule-conferring agencies such as schools, companies, etc. In this sense, as claims they have the force of 'must', even if they are not obeyed or if individuals dispute their legitimacy.

Obligation in a legal sense is a matter not of acceptance by those to whom it is applied but in the last instance of the capacity of those agencies advancing such claims to enforce them. Such enforcement may take many forms, not merely the police or prisons. The agencies in question may or may not have standing armies, police forces, prisons, etc., and this may or may not limit the credibility of their claims. Legitimacy is the knowledge that a rule being issued by the appropriate body is binding and obligatory: it makes the rule compelling. Hart's criticisms of Austin do not amount to a reduction of laws to guides to action. Whether it be the Holy Roman Empire or the Spanish Republican government-in-exile, an agency may make claims with differing degrees of success. The point is that, however inefficacious, such claims are coercive in the sense that they purport to be applicable to individuals and corporate bodies irrespective of any judgements of appropriateness the latter may make. They are externally binding and not merely accepted by those subject to them as a rule that morally or rationally governs their actions. Judgements of legitimacy by the agents subject to law are thus judgements of whether a rule is an obligatory one and not of whether one is obligated by it.

Thus Campbell's statement that he is talking of an 'untypical legal system' is true only if the rules in question are not analogous to a set of technical rules or a moral law (obligatory because of the rational or moral force they command), but have an extrinsic compelling character. Such a character is coercive and entails sanctions even if it may not involve the capacity to inflict physical punishment or rest on 'special bodies of armed men', in Lenin's phrase. Campbell cannot have his positivism and then reject it. If radical socialists cannot accept any rule that is extrinsic to the motivations of the individual and not merely a matter of rational or willed compliance – pleading that such rules are coercive and not a matter of consciously willed self-action – then they cannot accept a legal system. And a good deal of the revolutionary socialist objection to the 'coerciveness' of law as it is presented by Campbell amounts to this – not merely that law implies force, but that it violates autonomy and the acceptance of rules as intrinsic to their action by rational beings. Either Campbell must reduce law to a variant of moral law or technically rational rules, in which case his chosen socialist interlocutors will accept it, or he must accept a stronger *differentia specifica* for law and part company with the believers in an 'ideal' socialist system.

4 Socialism, Pluralism and Law

The object of this chapter is to argue that constitutional restraints on state authority are essential in socialist countries if they are to fulfil their aspirations to be less oppressive than capitalist ones, and that this conception of a socialist political order must influence the way in which socialist parties and political forces attempt to struggle for socialist objectives under Western parliamentary domocratic conditions.

In Chapter 2 I argued that it is time Marxists abandoned once and for all the myth of the 'withering away of the state' in the course of the transition to a communist society. This amounts to saying that communism is an unattainable ideal, that it is impossible to create a society enjoying the benefits of modern industry that does not have a constraining division of labour and in which the very 'administration of things' does not require political mechanisms for deciding between divergent interests and also forms of social control to support those decisions. It is now clear, as it was not at the end of the nineteenth century, that socialist societies can neither be run by command from a single centre, as in the authoritarian conception of a centrally planned economy, nor be run by the devolution of all power and decision-making to popular democratic bodies, as in the most extreme libertarian and syndicalist variants of socialism. *All* complex societies based on large-scale industry are necessarily 'pluralistic', in the limited sense that they involve many decision-making centres. At the same time, these centres' actions intermesh and they require means of coordination and regulation if they are not to conflict one with another and with the public interest. Planning institutions and modified market systems in combination provide such means of coordination, but their capacities need to be defined, and their actions regulated, by legal rules.

Laws are thus necessary in a socialist state both for economic efficiency and for the protection of citizens' interests and capacities for political action. This implies that institutions of regulation and review have some definite political autonomy, that they can check, rebuke and compel to desist or to make recompense powerful bodies like large enterprises, state agencies, etc. 'Pluralism' in the non-restricted sense – that is, a genuine diversity of autonomous social and political forces – is necessary if such elementary benefits of the 'bourgeois–liberal' era as freedom of public discussion, respect for the interests of minorities, etc., are to exist in the allegedly superior socialist form of society. It should be emphasized that such benefits are not some hangover from individualistic humanism, 'merely' a matter of human rights; rather they are a condition for rational and efficient economic decision-making and public policy-making.

The need for a framework of public law, in essence a working constitution, has been argued in Chapter 2 both to limit the power of state agencies and to enhance the quality of public policy-making. There is no doubt that efficiency suffers in countries like the USSR because information does not circulate freely and the consequences of decisions are not foreseen. To facilitate rational decision-making it is necessary that the interests involved be allowed to make their case, that the effects of decisions be thrashed out in debate and that, in the event of a genuine deadlock, the parties compromise or arbitration be utilized. At the same time, this implies constraints on political actors and their acceptance of the norms of a political culture based on discussion, agreement and compromise. It implies that political actors such as ministries, police and armed services abide by procedural rules and submit themselves to review. It implies that parties (including opposition parties), institutions of judicial review, representative institutions, and news media enjoy at least as great a political autonomy as they do in the West, but are also subject to the constraints of higher standards of honesty and respect for others' positions than currently exist in 'best practice' democracies.

Such a constitution would mean that social change had to proceed by debate and consent. It entails that the construction of an advanced liberal society and the socialization of the relations of production proceed together. Authoritarian 'forced march' social change is therefore rejected. As such, the earlier chapter involved some restrictions of scope. Its approach was evidently not directly applicable to 'primary socialist accumulation' under conditions of rural poverty and low productivity, but even here the cautions against authoritarianism and against irrationally forcing the pace of (pseudo) social change are relevant. Equally, it could offer few pointers to those struggling against anti-socialist dictatorships.

In envisaging such a constitution for a socialist society there are two obvious political points of reference: the first is the democratic reform of East European socialist states, were that to become possible; and the second is the attempt to build democratic socialism under parliamentary institutions in an advanced Western country. As a criticism of the authoritarian political regime of a command economy or as a demonstration of the defects of the notion of a 'commune state', the earlier chapter has served its purpose. It tried to point to the need for a complex institutional structure that would be more than liberal pluralism grafted on to centralized state socialism, and that would be an attempt to address the defects of traditional liberalism and Marxist socialism. These defects are, on the one hand, liberal constitutional restraints on state authority devised before the rise of big government, and, on the other, Marxist socialism in its Soviet version constructing authoritarian big government whilst claiming its system to be a 'people's democracy' that has no need for the obsolete devices of classical liberalism.

However, such a constitution as roughed-out in the earlier chapter assumed either a reformed Soviet-style socialism or a successful parliamentary democratic transition to socialism. It ignored the problems of getting there – legitimately enough to some extent, since its concern was to assess the feasibility of certain socialist objectives as social relations and not to consider the specific political means of getting to them. In the present chapter, I want to introduce two stern tests that need to be applied to this conception of a democratic socialist constitution if it is to have any political relevance and credibility. These tests are concerned with those aspects of the political world that appear to threaten a democratic system based on discussion, compromise and arbitration. The one concerns relations between states: to ask whether it is not the case that authoritarianism is built in to the state, socialist or otherwise, by its need to defend itself against others. The other concerns relations between political forces and social groups under pluralism: to ask whether under conditions of severe divergence of interests such political competition does not become so antagonistic as to have the potential of destroying the democratic framework in which those interests are able to compete. Such a divergence, it will be claimed, could well occur under capitalist democratic conditions where one party attempted with limited social support to construct a socialist economic system. The answers to both questions will be 'yes'. And yet, without paradox, I shall argue that this strengthens the demand for a democratic politics based on discussion and regulated by law.

To answer the first question. If it is true that within particular socialist countries there will, of necessity, be a plurality of agencies of decision-making and that these distinct capacities to arrive at objectives give rise to the possibility of conflicting interests, then the same follows for the international society in which these countries will exist. I have always been astounded that the 'one country' part of the slogan 'socialism in one country' has ever been questioned, as if there could be anything else but a world of states. Like other social agents, states will have interests and these may clash with those of other states. It has long been the hope of civilized statesmen that states be capable of settling their differences by arbitration or negotiation, and that they would forswear war as an instrument of policy. These hopes have not been realized and it is difficult to imagine the majority of states renouncing war in the near future. The number of states has grown with the dismantling of the great powers' colonial empires; the new nations are hungry to protect and extend their trappings of sovereignty – however meagre; and if there are established powers happy to restrict their use of war to the defence of what they have, there are also revisionist powers who would redraw boundaries if they could. Only the naive would expect this situation to change because a large number of those states are nominally 'socialist' or expect 'socialist' states not to fight one another.

It is true that the nuclear powers and their close allies are genuinely fearful of using war as an instrument of policy against one another – quite simply they fear such a war would become a nuclear one, and they know that a nuclear war would negate any conceivable objective the victor might have pursued. Nevertheless, such powers have not renounced war; rather they avoid *starting* wars. They coexist in a watchful armed peace without any genuine security as to others' intentions. This watchful armed peace is tantamount to what

Hobbes terms a 'a state of warre'. Lesser and less closely allied powers may not share this constraint and may indeed hope to benefit from war-as-policy. In truth one must add that some uses of armed force may still be regarded as 'just'. A depressing example of such a 'just war' is the Vietnamese invasion of Kampuchea: both states were nominally 'socialist', the Vietnamese were certainly pursuing narrow nationalist objectives, and yet they were driving out what was in substance a bestial tyranny and replacing it by some measure of order and respect for human life.

The point of the foregoing is simple: states are not merely 'governments' in the sense of means of coordinating and organizing the economic and social affairs of a particular area; they are also bodies that lay claim to govern that territory to a greater or lesser degree of exclusion of other parties. This claim may or may not amount to an absolute and inalienable 'sovereignty'; it is compatible with being bound by international and supra-state agencies' decisions in a wide range of areas (the UK, for example, submits to the decisions of various institutions such as the EEC or the European Court of Human Rights). This claim may or may not be issued and pursued in a bellicose manner; it may or may not involve a large standing army – as the example of Switzerland shows. It does involve, however, the possibility of a state a war, and with such a state a substantial and obligating claim by the state on the lives and property of its citizens. All states have the capacity to declare a state of emergency or war, and to compel citizens in quite draconian ways and with precious little redress. That interstate relations still approximate to a watchful armed peace means that all states, however democratic, humane and pacific their leaders and citizens may wish to be, contain within them Hobbes' sovereign public power. No socialist, whatever his or her aspirations, should forget this fact. At the worst, the military and the accompanying apparatus of internal surveillance and state security may crush all autonomous politics and abrogate to themselves the major decisions as to economic and social policies.

To answer the second question is more difficult. Chapter 2 said virtually nothing about how we actually get to a democratic socialism. A pluralistic socialist system appears to be a desirable general objective, but in particular instances it raises the thorny problem of who is to be or can be part of the plurality and who not?

In particular, how are parties and political forces that fundamentally reject socialist goals to be treated? An attempt to socialize an advanced Western economy would, in all probability, test that institutional framework to breaking point. Socialization is unlikely to be a matter of consensus and will challenge actors' commitment to democratic procedural values in political life. Otto Kirchheimer contended that

> [such a] democracy provides a crucible for the crosscurrents and encounters of classes and their value systems, in which, to be more precise, the antagonistic forces are lined up at a particular stage of the class struggle. This poses the question as to how government is at all possible under such conditions and who decides who are the wielders of governmental power. In the case of a democracy characterised by agreement on fundamental values, a majority vote amounts to a decision on the best way to concretise these common values. In the absence of such basic agreement it is by no means self-evident why the majority should have the power to decide, for in that case majority rule is tantamount to passive submission of the minority to its political opponents. [Kirchheimer, 1969, pp. 5–6]

The traditional answer to this problem among Marxists has been to regard the issue as one of the militant resistance of the capitalists and their class allies to socialization and to see the answer in some form of the 'dictatorship of the proletariat'. When Marx coined the phrase, the world was innocent of modern dictatorships, be they nominally 'socialist' or otherwise, and dictatorship was conceived by him on the Roman model of an emergency and temporary authority to preserve the republic in a state of crisis. To use Carl Schmitt's (1976) distinction, it was a 'commissarial dictatorship' in form, even if its function was that of a 'sovereign dictatorship'.[1] It is also the case that Marx supposed the proletariat would form the immense mass of the population and would be united against a small minority of undemocratic exploiters and oppressors. The people-in-arms would exercise these emergency powers and would naturally enough cease to utilize them when the oppressors were vanquished.

We have no excuse to remain in Marx's condition of innocence. Marx conceived of politics before the existence of modern big government or organized mass political parties. He wrote of a capitalism where it was just possible to imagine the industrial manual workers would form a majority, sharing a common condition of life such that they could act with unity. Today we cannot even have the illusion that Marx's 'proletariat' exists in advanced industrial capitalism. The productivity and efficiency of modern industry have made industrial manual workers a minority of the labour force in the West, and employment in manufacturing in general is nowhere even half of the labour force. The complexities of economic administration and the rise of a large health, education and welfare sector have created a large 'middle class' salariat. The rise in living standards based on industrial productivity has made possible a large marketed-services sector that would defy efficient 'socialization' and yet is valued by consumers who have ample spare income and leisure time after the necessaries of life have been earned.

Since Bernstein's *Evolutionary Socialism* was written at the turn of the last century, it has been clear that Western capitalist economies were destined to remain socially pluralistic; that 'proletarianization' – in the sense of a mass levelling of incomes and conditions – would not take place. Bernstein showed that the propertied middle classes – the peasant small landowners, the small businessmen, etc. – in Germany formed the social base of a veto group that could prevent revolution and socialism. Today the same is even more true of a Western industrial country like the UK. Millions own property and financial assets, hundreds of thousands own, run or share in small businesses, and almost everybody except the poorest of the poor enjoys the freedom of consumption made possible by a large marketed-services sector of the economy. Unlike Germany or Britain in 1899, when socialism represented the hope of a better future, today citizens of Western Germany or the UK can see that the USSR does not provide the same freedoms of economic action and consumption, leaving aside the question of authoritarian political relations.[2]

Even if we were to accept the most simplistic vulgar-Marxist assumption that people know and pursue their class interests, we should have to conclude that millions of 'petits bourgeois' will oppose socialism, if socialism is a system run by and for the 'proletariat'. Actually, the conditions of the majority of salaried and waged workers in Western societies in no sense resemble '*les damnés de la terre*', who have 'nothing to lose but their chains'. Even a devotee of simplistic economism would have to conclude that Western societies are and will remain socially and politically pluralistic.

In fact, Western politics refuse to reduce themselves to class terms, whether the question be party allegiances or the dominant political issues. Many industrial and manual workers vote for parties of the Right, sections of the salariat for the Left, and in Italy sections of the peasantry for the Communists. If the classic Marxist classes, as defined by their relationship to the means of production, fit the social and political topography of the Western world rather badly, so too do more conventional 'class' categories based on levels of skill and income.

Bernstein was loathed for stating the obvious; not for his cautious, revisionist, democratic socialism, which most of his opponents, quite rightly, shared in substance. He upset the new social democratic orthodoxy-in-the-making which magicked away the problems of how to get a socialist parliamentary majority and the means of then imposing socialist rule. This was accomplished by means of the theory of 'twofold progress'. According to this theory, economic progress would automatically confer a position of social majority on the working class, and when this became a political majority the bourgeoisie would submit gracefully because it accepted, along with the general development of civilization, humanitarian and democratic values.[3]

Kautsky, Bernstein's most rigorous social democratic opponent, realized the parliamentary socialists might have to use force against determined extra-legal action by opponents but that this would be both legitimate and popular.[4] Kautsky contended in *The Dictatorship of the Proletariat* (1918) that the advent of modern parliamentary democracy had taken the sting out of the dictatorship of the proletariat. Kautsky rejected dictatorship as a 'form of government' – the socialist transitional government would remain a *Rechtsstaat* – but he envisaged it as a 'political condition', that is, an overwhelming majority vote that would confer legitimacy on the lawful actions of the government. The proletariat would become the 'ruling class' – in the sense of electing and supporting a government that pursued its interests and not in the sense of directly imposing itself by armed force in the streets. From Engels' (1895) 'Introduction' to Marx's *The*

Class Struggles in France, intelligent Marxist socialists had realized that the old popular revolutionary tradition was finished in Western Europe. The armed forces and the administrative power of the modern state could shatter any popular attempt at a *coup d'état*. Kautsky's realism extended to insurrectionary but not to parliamentary politics: his dictatorship as a 'political condition' is as improbable as that of the people-in-arms. First, parties committed to radical and rapid socialization are unlikely even to get 51 per cent of the popular vote, a narrow legitimacy at best for such sweeping changes in terms of parliamentary values. Secondly, the opposition is unlikely to succumb to the 'accident' of a socialist victory at the polls and forswear extra-parliamentary and illegal struggle.

To the degree that a government committed to socialization is *possible* under contemporary Western parliamentary conditions, it will face the challenge of 'antagonistic pluralism'. 'Antagonistic pluralism' is a condition where the differentiation and divergence of social forces, pursuing incompatible conceptions of social relations, is both facilitated by, and also threatens to wreck, democratic institutions. In the no-holds-barred struggle of contending political and social forces, the opposing parties will use the procedural and legal framework when convenient, but refuse to be bound by it in any genuine sense. The degree to which such a government is possible and the degree of resistance to it will, in part, depend on the type and pace of socialization proposed: a coalition of socialist political forces that is sincerely committed to extending democratic mechanisms and to limiting big government's powers, that does not try to socialize small enterprises or owner-occupied housing, that consults and does not seek to forge ahead regardless of opposition, and so on, is more likely to be permitted to govern. But one should not be too optimistic; the degree of radicalism and the degree of resistance to it have no rational ratio. Many decent and sensible people have a powerful and almost unconscious fear of socialism, a fear that may drive them to desperate opposition. Given the spectre of Stalin, one can understand the fear that socialization will undermine the genuine social pluralism that makes political democracy possible.

'Antagonistic pluralism' is a condition by no means confined to the scenario of a democratic socialist government confronted with opponents who treat the rules as at best a convenience. It can exist where *no* party has a majority and perhaps *several* of them pose actual or potential challenges of different kinds to the existing order. If Chile under Allende is a good example of the first scenario, the Weimar Republic in the period from Bruning to von Papen is a good example of the latter.

Such situations pose, in Carl Schmitt's terms, the 'challenge of the exception'.[5] Otto Kirchheimer, a democratic Marxist confronted by the turmoil of Weimar, went so far as to claim: 'Of fundamental importance for every political theory is the position which it adopts toward the concept of dictatorship, to what extent it takes account of, and admits into its texture, the principle of emergency' (Kirchheimer, 1969, p. 14). Schmitt's answer to such 'exceptional' conditions of antagonistic pluralism was a commissarial dictatorship; this was quite unlike Marx's in function since it was exercised by, or on behalf of, the authoritative source in the state charged with the defence of the constitution. Schmitt is clear that the task of such a dictatorship is to decide who – within the polity – is friend and who enemy. Such a commissarial dictatorship uses its power to suppress the enemies of the constitution, with greater or lesser use of force and suspension of civil rights depending on the concrete situation. Such a dictatorship is essentially conservative, even when exercised by a nominally 'socialist' head of state like Ebert. A 'sovereign dictatorship', on the other hand, is in no sense bound by the existing constitution; it seeks to reconstitute political relationships and is in no way limited by pre-existing constitutional law. In terms of this classification, Marx's dictatorship was a hybrid. As we have seen, it was conceived as temporary and emergency power on the Roman model, but it had unlimited and revolutionary aims. It was also exercised by a class, acting for itself, and not some constitutionally empowered political agency.

Given that *classes* can as such neither rule nor govern (only specific political organizations can do this), then the 'dictatorship of the proletariat' must actually mean exceptional powers utilized by political forces acting through state apparatuses to suppress those defined as enemies. We are familiar with this definition through and through: it describes Stalin's Terror and all the lesser terrors exercised in the name of liberation from oppression and exploitation. What is disconcerting about Schmitt's analysis is that the definition we have given of dictatorship as 'exceptional powers utilized by political forces acting through state apparatuses to suppress those defined as enemies' applies generally to *all* examples of the state of exception. It fits a moderate 'socialist' president trying to cope with antagonistic pluralism. It is only the degree to which the concrete situation permits moderation and the conservative goals of the commissarial dictatorship that limit its use of terror. As in the case of socialism in a world of states, we have reached back in our analysis to a Hobbesian premise. The 'exception' again reveals the state not as merely a 'government' but as a power that claims to be the dominant source of binding rules within a territory, that determines who is friend or foe within that territory, and that attempts to substantiate that claim if need be by force.

Schmitt's 'decisionism' is all too likely to be used against radical socialist forces by established authority and to compromise socialism in that way, but it is equally capable of being used *by* them when they attain state power and thus compromise socialism in another and more damaging way. This dilemma cannot be solved either by the phrase the 'dictatorship of the proletariat' or by socialists eschewing the actual conditions denoted by it and resolving always to be democratic, for emergency powers may be used against or have to be used by a democratic socialist parliamentary party.

Hobbes and Marx, Carl Schmitt and Lenin, strange bedfellows, show us that state power is in essence dictatorial. They reveal what the liberal tradition, with its emphasis on constitutional restraints on state authority, often seems to forget in a reverie of a politics based on discussion, consent and the rule of law – that political struggle always involves the possibility of friend–enemy relations and the use of force. I do not mean by saying that state power is 'in essence' dictatorial that it is normally exercised by a dictatorship, or that it normally takes the form of lawless arbitrary power. The challenge of the exception is that it reveals what 'normality' hides – antagonistic political struggle and its resolution by force sanctioned by a claim to lawfulness. State power is dictatorial in the sense that Clausewitz argues that absolute war – the unlimited use of all potentially available force – is the essence of war. Political struggle and war both entail 'reciprocal action' and, therefore, the potential of an ascent to extremes. The containment of such struggle in the state, the maintenance of 'civil peace', may involve the use of armed force as sanctioned and legitimated by the claim to lawfulness. 'Order' cannot exclude force; 'civil peace' cannot exclude a decision as to who is enemy.

Carl Schmitt attended Max Weber's seminar in Munich in 1919–20. Clearly he learned much from the man whose work he subjected to critical dialogue;[6] for it was Weber who defined the nature of modern state power most accurately. Weber's definition is as follows:

> It possesses an administrative and legal order subject to change by legislation, to which the organized activities of the administrative staff, which are also controlled by regulations, are oriented. This system of order claims binding authority, not only over the members of the state, the citizens, most of whom have obtained membership by birth, but also to a very large extent over all action taking place in the area of its jurisdiction. *It is thus a compulsory organization with a territorial basis.* Furthermore, today, the use of force is regarded as legitimate only so far as it is either permitted by the state or prescribed by it . . . *The claim of the modern state to monopolize the use of force is as essential to it as its character of compulsory jurisdiction and of continuous operation.* [1978, Vol. 1, p. 56; my emphasis]

Weber correctly presents the state as an entity making a series of *claims*: to a definite territory, as to who is subject to it, and to be the source of obligatory rules backed by sanctions. The claim to lawfulness and the claim to a monopoly of force are combined and conditional one upon another. The latter substantiates the former and the former legitimates and makes effective the latter as a special class of claim. State power is inescapable authority in the sense that it is obligatory and, if effective, is backed by sanctions that in turn may involve the use of force. State power is exclusive authority in that it claims a monopoly of sanction-stipulating norms and of whatever means are used to sanction. The state in Weber's definition is a *Rechtsstaat* in the 'formal' sense, in that its actions take place according to legal rules, but nothing is said of the substantive nature of those rules. Indeed, the claim to 'monopolize the use of force' entails both the state of war and the state of exception. The series of claims by which Weber defines the state clearly specify the use of armed force as a sanction, legitimated by the claim to lawfulness. They imply the condition of dictatorship as surely as Lenin's or Trotsky's conception of the state as ultimately bodies of armed men securing the rule of a class.

Weber's use of this series of claims makes clear the nature of sovereignty: the state presents itself as a single dominant public power. However much it may actually be composed of an unruly congeries of institutions, jurisdictions and decision-making centres, the state claims to be a single sovereign dominion. In practice, definite bodies must claim to speak or act in the name of that power. The point and value of Schmitt's 'decisionism' is to ask who or what claims to speak in its name. Whoever speaks in the name of the sovereign constituted power may take the measures necessary to preserve the existence of the state, to substantiate its claims; measures that are permitted by its rules and are consistent with the restoration of its authority. In this sense, state power is dictatorship in the form of law. Indeed, as far as its recipients are concerned, the *claim* that differentiates law from other classes of rule – that of being obligatory, compelling and without legitimate competitor – is dictatorial. It permits of no challenge that does not make its issuer an enemy. 'Democratic' states are in this respect as dictatorial as undemocratic ones. 'Democracy' here means that those qualified to vote can participate in choosing some of the personnel of the bodies that make the claims outlined above.

We have seen that democratic socialism faces two challenges. First, as the government of a state it will find itself potentially in opposition to others and must make provision (as a minimum) for the defence of its territory. It will thus have the potential to make obligatory demands on the life and property of its citizens in war. Secondly, in so far as socialization involves radical changes in social relations that challenge established interests, democratic socialism faces the prospect of antagonistic political struggle. At best this may mean a socialist government may use legally constituted state power to resist extra-legal action and receives majority support in so doing. Even so, it is using its position to determine who is an enemy within the political system and taking measures to neutralize that enemy. Political relations that involve struggle against opposing forces constituted as 'enemies' – wars between states and emergency situations within their own territories – involve the 'dictatorial' use of power. Socialist parties and organizations, however pacifist and democratic in aspiration, cannot rely on decision-making based solely upon discussion and agreement.

One cannot avoid the 'challenge of the exception' or the potentiality of friend–enemy relations in the 'reciprocal action' that is political struggle. To the extent that the revolutionary Marxist tradition recognized those realities, it exploited them for polemical purposes but failed to apply them critically to its own conception of the future society. Revolutionary Marxists used their theories of the inevitability of antagonistic class struggle and the dictatorial class power present (if more or less hidden) in every form of state to insist on the necessity of an insurrection and to reject as fatuous the idea of a 'parliamentary road' to socialism. This pillorying of the democratic Marxist socialists of the Second International needs to be challenged for what it was – successful propaganda based on half-truth. Actually, there were and have been few believers in a painless parliamentary socialism. On the contrary, democratic socialists like Kautsky were at least willing to sanction the use of legitimate force to defeat undemocratic opposition. This was not merely a slogan but was carried out in practice; thus, for example, the social democratic state government in Prussia in 1932 tried to use its public order and police powers to check Nazi street violence – only to be removed by the Reich government. Democratic socialists have also resisted the use of authoritarian measures to declare them 'enemies of the state' and eliminate them by force – for example, the Austrian socialists' *Schützbund* which offered armed resistance to the fascist attack upon them in 1934.

In fact, it was the great fault of utopian, rather than parliamentary, socialism to ignore these realities. The utopians were not merely unworldly about the means needed to bring their perfect futures into being, they also envisaged them as a non-political and non-pluralist form of society, without even the potential for antagonistic interests. Communism is exactly such a society and, whilst Marx and Engels vigorously opposed the utopians' naivety and contended that socialism could only be established by struggle and force, they also believed that in the eventual stage of communism such things would have gradually disappeared. However much blood might have been shed on the road to utopia, political struggle and bloodletting had no place there. This utopian end-state crippled realistic Marxist thinking about socialism as a form of society and made the 'dictatorship of the proletariat' appear tolerable as a brief interlude on the way to a better future. Take away utopia, and dictatorship must be faced for what it is, a condition potentially present in all state power. Far from making the defence of democratic institutions and the elaboration of constitutional limits on state power appear naive and unrealistic – 'parliamentary cretinism' to use the sneering phrase – the 'challenge of the exception' makes them ever more necessary. It is the revolutionary Marxist embrace of a (temporary) dictatorship (exercised by the people themselves) that is the chimera; it leads in practice not to a libertarian stateless future but to 'people's states' – something Marx ridiculed as a contradiction in terms when proposed by certain of the utopians.

There is an attempt to avoid the logic of the foregoing argument which merits serious attention, which questions that state power *is* inevitable and which seeks to avoid the authoritarian dangers built in to the very conception of the 'dictatorship of the proletariat'. G. D. H. Cole – the principal theorist of the British guild socialists – tried to construct a vision of a socialism without the state, thus avoiding the defects of both Marxism and anarchism. Cole sought to be practical, to think out details of socialist social organization without being utopian. He began by questioning the need for the state and asking whether in practice the modern state could justify its claims to be the primary source of political obligation. Using the work of John Figgis and Harold Laski, Cole challenged the modern notion of 'sovereignty' and its foundation in doctrines of representative democracy. The state is 'sovereign', is a single public power to which the citizen owes primary obligation, because it is claimed it represents the will of the people in a democratically elected representative assembly. Cole challenged this idea of 'representativeness': in actuality an elected representative cannot possibly represent the wills and interests of all the electors or even the ones who voted for him.

Cole argued instead for a pluralistic political system, without a single dominant source of authority. This system would be based on 'functional democracy', that is, that individuals would be free to choose what obligations to accept and what activities to be involved in according to their particular interests. Activities would be run by self-management and direct democracy, and association would be a matter of individuals choosing to come together. Associations would work out means of coordination and would resolve differences by agreement.[7]

It will be recalled that this doctrine of functional democracy was criticized in Chapter 2: it was pointed out that this doctrine either restores central coordinating authority in all but name, or must make unwarranted assumptions about the natural harmony of interests. But not only does functional democracy raise problems of coordination in the sphere of 'government' decision-making in the realm of day-to-day economic and social administration, it simply ignores friend–enemy relations in politics altogether and the necessities of compulsion of individuals' membership of associations that arise from antagonistic political struggle. The claim to obligatoriness, that one *must* obey rather than choose to join in, is utterly ignored in this theory. It is not only states that make this claim; any political body that requires discipline in order to be capable of struggling does so – trade unions demand loyalty and solidarity, for example.

Cole's was a syndicalist socialism that imagined a gentlemanly world in which associations are like clubs, which one may join or not as one pleases. States differ from other organizations in making grander claims, but all associations that must engage in struggle demand loyalty and obedience from their members and seek to enforce it. Otto Kirchheimer's remarks sum up the defects of this type of pluralist theory all too well:

> In the pluralists' zealous endeavours to destroy the image of the centralised state and to install the free reign of the voluntary groups on its ruins with a kind of vast 'super clearing-house' as a coordinating agency, social reality of group life in industrial society was invariably romanticised. It is one thing to harmonise relations between different clubs which may be indiscriminately and simultaneously joined by the same individuals; it is an entirely different matter to harmonise the life of mutually exclusive groups. [1969, p. 161]

Having introduced two stern tests, it might be thought that a democratic socialism in which 'the construction of an advanced liberal society and the socialization of the relations of production proceed together' is simply absurd. Surely, it must join the myth of 'twofold progress' on the garbage heap where all social democratic illusions belong? In fact, the contrary is true. It is the 'dictatorship of the proletariat' that is a myth. For the 'proletariat' there can only be substitutes and these substitutes will encounter opposition from other social forces such that, if they persist in their aims, they must turn to brutality. If there can only ever be 'national' socialisms, then a socialist state, however powerful and however determined, will encounter force that it is useless to challenge in war. The USSR learnt both these lessons long ago; it has become a shambling, bureaucratic, semi-*Rechtsstaat*, and a profoundly conservative rather than a revolutionary power in foreign policy.

What the USSR has been unable to do is to face its own predicament and reform its economy and polity. It has also prevented its satellite allies from taking noisy steps in that direction, although it has tolerated quiet progress in countries like Hungary. The USSR is neither a lawless tyranny nor a totalitarian autocracy – it is a society suffering advanced bureaucratico-sclerosis, recognized by its own leaders to be in need of reforms to promote efficiency and accountability, and semi-paralysed by the fear of change.

The myth of the 'dictatorship of the proletariat' appears a superficially realistic answer to the inherent authoritarianism of state power outlined above. In fact, it merely accentuates these built-in tendencies, in the illusion either that this will be temporary or that it will be popular democratic. In this chapter I have used Schmitt's opposition between a conception of politics based on 'discussion' (bourgeois parliamentary liberalism) and politics based on an authority that stabilizes friend–enemy relations. This is useful in its way for it does expose a real tendency to blindness about force and struggle in the nineteenth-century liberal constitutional and the democratic socialist traditions. It is, however, an opposition that it would be stupid to accentuate by considering either pole to be the more desirable or realistic. Schmitt contributed to the denigration of a politics built on discussion because his narrow Hobbesian view of power ultimately led him to accept Hitler as a source of order against chaos. Struggle alone, friend–enemy relations, cannot solve all political problems. Discussion and orderly agreement are two of the conditions of long-term efficiency in decision-making. Advanced societies cannot be made to run like a Crusade or their members turned into the homogeneous components of an ideal social order. On the other hand, neither can discussion alone always settle political questions where interests diverge. However, building a political system where interests are accommodated, if possible, where policy is based on discussion (and, if not agreement, then the knowledge of the consequences of overriding opposed interests), is an essential task. Western democracies approximate to such a political system to different degrees and on different dimensions.

In fact, the two tests I have imposed confirm rather than refute the necessity of the attempt to disperse and control state power and to give adequate reflection to social pluralism in a stable political pluralism. Such pluralism may not be 'liberal' in the conventional sense, for, like socialism, nineteenth-century liberalism pre-dated the rise of 'big government' and is ill-adapted to place restraints upon it. Representative democracy is a weak system for the detailed supervision of state power: in British-style systems, the election of representatives provides members for both the heads of ministries and the legislature; in other systems a division is made, for example the highest executive post and the legislature are elected separately. Legislatures cannot tackle the manifold decisions of the multiform administrative machine. 'Big government' is an unwieldy congeries of different agencies. Likewise ministers or presidents are substantively no more than the titular heads of a vast continuing decision-making apparatus. To control this, other bodies specifically empowered and possessing adequate knowledge are required: supervising tribunals, administrative courts, inspectorates, etc.

A common spectre of free-market liberals and socialists alike is 'corporatism', but genuinely knowledgeable and effective representation of 'interests' may involve just this at national, local and organizational levels. In fact, popular 'interests' have the most to gain from a corporate system, since those well-endowed with wealth, information and power will have adequate means of informal 'corporate' influence. I tried to outline some of these elements of a polity designed to supervise 'big government' in Chapter 2, but one non-starter as the *primary* means of doing so is 'popular democracy'. Representative and popular democracy both have a place in an 'advanced liberal society'. Representative democracy ensures minimum political rights for all citizens only if the body to which they elect personnel is of some consequence in the political system. Popular democracy where it *can* work, as enterprise and local-level self-management, is valuable as low-cost administration, as a political training ground, and as a bedrock of political pluralism. It cannot, however, replace representative democracy or control of administration by specialists; it is a valuable and invigorating supplement to a polity but can never form its core. Specialists are often derided as bureaucrats and professionals, but a complexly administered society demands informed personnel with the autonomy to monitor and check the actions of its bureaucracies.

In fact, such autonomy, not merely for courts or inspectors but for a wide variety of political bodies, is a precondition of genuine political pluralism. However much the state may and must present itself as a single public power, that power must be delegated and diffused in order to be exercised, but this differentiation of decision-making agencies is common to *all* modern states, Nazi Germany included. Political pluralism proper means two things:

(1) that most of the significant social interests find representation in the political system;
(2) that the political system itself has multiple centres and these are connected with the different state decision-making agencies, and that therefore important decisions are considered and influenced by more than one source of interest.

In this latter sense, the 'pluralist' critique of Cole *et al.* had some point to it, as had the classic liberal constitutional doctrine of the 'separation of powers'. An 'advanced liberal society' would need to minimize the degree to which a very few centres within the state could legitimately utter the 'claims' that define it. It would thus disperse 'sovereignty' – the capacity to determine friend and foe within and without – to a number of distinct bodies. For example, to declare a 'state of emergency' it would be necessary not merely for a representative assembly to approve it, but also, say, a constitutional court. Such a 'state' would need to be precisely specified in terms of the conditions under which it was appropriate, of the rights to be suspended and of the capacities of state agencies that were thereby enhanced. The more real power centres in a polity and the more the dispersal of the capacity to enunciate such claims, the greater the chance of checking the dictatorial tendencies inherent in state power.

Political and social pluralism cannot easily be divorced. Autonomous political bodies and forces ultimately depend on the existence of distinct social forces with capacities for independent political action. Such forces exist *in potentia* in all advanced societies based on large-scale industry. Their number can be reduced by exclusion from the formal channels of political influence, and by dispersal and disarticulation by police action. Indeed, all societies do this to some extent; some 'interests' are bound to be regarded as anathema. Social pluralism implies two things:

(1)　that a reasonable degree of latitude be permitted to the formation of interest groups and self-administering groups by the political system – not merely protest groups, pressure groups, 'issue organizations', etc., but also associations, clubs, voluntary bodies, and so on;[8]
(2)　that this be underlain by the toleration of genuine differences on local, occupational, ethnic and other dimensions.

A democratic socialism that used modified market mechanisms for a wide range of goods and services, that recognized various property forms (such as cooperatives, private ownership for small businesses, etc.), and that accepted a diversity of cultures and lifestyles would guarantee this latter aspect of social pluralism. For this reason, the conception of 'socialism' as a social system organized on a single principle is a disaster; the pursuit of a classless, non-commodity society can only lead to treating all existing sources of social differentiation as at best a fact to be compromised with. The Marxist conception of 'modes of production', of societies as 'totalities' ultimately governed by their economic relationships, is a clear example of this. Social pluralism is not a compromise with regrettable facts, it is something to be constructed. It does not mean the same thing as the 'mixed economy', where in practice there is no 'mix' since corporate capitalist big battalions and bureaucratic nationalized industries predominate.[9]

If the objective of political and social forces committed to socialization is a democratic socialism, with political and social pluralism, then this needs to be fought for in a way compatible with the objective. There is *no* parliamentary 'road' to socialism, no historically emergent path as in the illusory theory of 'twofold progress'. There is no foolproof way of avoiding 'antagonistic pluralism' or the use of authoritarian state power. However, to articulate a conception of socialism in which social and political pluralism are part of the objective, not concessions until we get something else, may increase its popular appeal. Likewise, to exercise restraint in political struggle, to insist on the values of discussion and respect for political opponents, may not guarantee political success, but it will prevent defeat in a more profound sense.

NOTES

1   For a full account of Schmitt's distinction see Schwab (1970).

2   Which is not to imply the USSR and its allies in Eastern Europe are accurately perceived or living conditions in Soviet-style economies thoroughly understood by ordinary people in the UK. The GDR, for example, has a higher GDP per capita than the UK, and it has neither mass unemployment nor an underclass living in grinding poverty. Inaccurate and as influenced by the gutter press as mass perceptions may be about many aspects of Soviet life, people's perceptions are accurate about the *real* shortcomings of the Soviet system – the relative lack of civil liberties and the relative lack of choice in consumption. These are also the things that critical citizens – who are neither Soviet placemen nor disaffected émigrés – find wrong with the Soviet system.

3   For an examination of this theory of 'twofold progress' see Otto Kirchheimer, 'The Socialist and Bolshevik Theory of the State' (1928) in Kirchheimer (1969).

4   Kautsky's complex and changing views are telescoped here. In *The Road to Power* (1909), Kautsky took a relatively radical view of the struggle for socialism. Later, in *The Dictatorship of the Proletariat* (1918), he opposed Lenin's view of the Bolshevik Revolution, insisting on the need to build a democratic majority based on the full development and maturation of the proletariat. Socialism demanded prolonged political work and the formation of an advanced capitalist industrial system. Kautsky did not, however, imagine that a democratic majority would ensure a peaceful transition. For an accessible collection of excerpts from Kautsky's work see Patrick Goode (ed.) (1983) and for a political biography Gary P. Steenson (1979).

5   Carl Schmitt has an odious reputation: a brilliant constitutional lawyer and legal theorist in the Weimar Republic, he provided justification for the authoritarian conservative 'presidential' forces and for the use of emergency powers by von Schleicher and von Papen. After Hitler's nomination as Chancellor, he flirted with the Nazis, only to fall from

grace and to be forced into virtual political silence after 1936. I have no time for people who try to resurrect forgotten thinkers of the ultra–Right simply because they were clever. Schmitt merits the odium heaped upon him. Unfortunately, aspects of his work are too important to leave in obscurity: he addresses the problems of antagonistic pluralism, emergency powers and constitutional dictatorship in a manner nowhere available in the liberal and Marxist traditions. He could be said to have applied the Hobbesian conception of the state to the problems of modern constitutional plebiscitarian democracies. Before his cynical endorsement of Nazism, he was respected by serious Left legal theorists such as Franz Neumann and Schmitt's former pupil Otto Kirchheimer, and regarded as a serious opponent by traditional conservatives like Leo Strauss. For a biography of Schmitt see Bendersky (1983), for an account of his thought in the period 1921–36 see Schwab (1970) and for a brilliant example of his political theory, outlining his 'friend–enemy' thesis, see *The Concept of the Political* (1976).

6 See Schwab (1970), p. 28. I make no apology for citing Weber. I have strongly criticized the theoretical foundations of Weber's political theory but it would be a rationalist error to suppose the whole of his work to be no more than a necessary extension of its methodological doctrines – see Hirst (1976). I find Weber's definition of the modern state accurate and compelling, but this is no way commits one to the other definitions in *Economy and Society*.

7 For characteristic examples of Cole's argument see *The Social Theory* (1921) and *Self-Government in Industry* (1917). Cole's guild socialism ideas are sympathetically outlined and discussed in Wright (1979) and his controversy with the Webbs about the constitution of a socialist system in Tomlinson (1982), ch. 3.

8 The role of 'secondary associations' in sustaining a pluralistic political system has been a commonplace since Alexis de Tocqueville. It is by no means the case that in accepting the necessity of social pluralism one must accept Tocqueville's anti-socialist and conservative politics. Only if one conceives socialism as a monolithic centrally planned economy without differentiated decision-making agencies, and as a society with a complete homogeneity of living conditions and values, would that be the case. Gavin Kitching in *Re-Thinking Socialism* (1983) has argued persuasively why an actively organized and differentiated 'civil society' is an essential condition for a democratic socialism.

9 The conception of socialism as a society governed by a single principle, as a 'totality', has dogged Marxist socialists. It leads to the notion of a post-political society devoid of differences of interests and, therefore,

without the need for mechanisms whereby these interests can be expressed and reconciled. In the name of a popular democratic general will it gives rise to a system that gives precious little say to the actual populace and that insulates the state machine against the demands of its citizens. For an excellent discussion of the paradoxical outcome of Marxist political theory see Tony Polan (1984).

5 Extending Democracy

It is often assumed that a democratic or parliamentary socialism will adopt a passive and conservative approach to the representative institutions by means of which it has come to power. It is evident that the conditions of stable parliamentary politics in advanced Western countries will deny victory at the ballot box to any party that seeks the revolutionary overthrow of the existing constitutional and legal framework. Few democratic socialists would wish to do so even if they could, fearing that the result would be a dictatorship and one-party domination. But democratic socialist ideas are virtually meaningless if they do not encompass the radical reform of the political system by legal means, including the reform of Parliament itself. Political reforms – such as radical democratization – ought to be as important as economic and social reforms to democratic socialists today. Indeed, they ought to perceive that democratization is one of the preconditions for the lasting success of socialist policies.

It is the measure of the diminution and retreat of our claims and objectives that we leave existing forms of representative democracy unchallenged and untouched. The only beneficiaries of this evacuation of a vital terrain of struggle are our political opponents; our silence reinforces the *status quo*. In the 1920s, democratic socialists were far from silent on the question of representative democracy and its reform. In Weimar Germany, elements in the SPD advanced the concept of a *'sozialer Rechtsstaat'*, a deepening and extension of democracy in the area of social and welfare rights. In democratic Britain, socialists like G. D. H. Cole and the Webbs proposed very different but equally radical reforms of the political structure. Democrats did not cling to representative democracy and the political philosophy of liberalism in quite the same way that so much of the European parliamentary Left does today. Representative democracy and parliamentary sovereignty were challenged conceptually and politically – read the early works of Cole and Laski and measure the difference from our deferential endorsement of the *status quo*.[1]

Why are we so timid? Because when Cole, Laski and the Webbs proposed their radical criticisms the world was still innocent of fascist and Soviet dictatorships. We have defended representative democracy, liberal individual rights and political pluralism because the *status quo* was much better than these very real alternatives to it. Our caution has outlived the threats and become second nature. The absence of radical voices against the political *status quo* means that any attempt to propose far-reaching reforms of representative institutions will be seized upon by our conservative opponents. But fascist mass parties and militant Leninist parties with mass support no longer exist in Western Europe. The threat to democratic values and processes is no longer external, but inherent in the existing representative parliamentary system – in its minimization of political objectives and its depoliticization through under-participation.

To counter this threat we cannot simply put the clock back and return to the classics of democratic socialism, to Cole or to Karl Kautsky. Cole and Kautsky were naive in the 1920s; confronted with modern 'big government' they are hopelessly out of date. But so is our current practice. Parliamentarism and representative democracy are a creation of nineteenth-century liberalism struggling to cope with the political realities of the late twentieth century.

The assumption that reform is something that happens outside the Palace of Westminster has certainly bitten deep into the Labour Party. Hostile Marxist critics like Ralph Miliband in his ironically entitled *Parliamentary Socialism* (1964) disputed that the party could ever be a vehicle of genuine social change. If one reads an enthusiastic supporter of parliamentary ritual and cautious piecemeal reform like Herbert Morrison, one might actually imagine Miliband was right. It is difficult to imagine a more complacent and apologetic book than *Government and Parliament* (1954). Morrison may be dead, but the real source of his complacency isn't and is in fact shared by people far to the left of him. Labour governments have concentrated on *using* existing parliamentary and administrative means to deliver social reforms and economic benefits rather than on changing the machinery of representation and administration. This has been good practical politics; the British electorate has had no enthusiasm for the sort of change Miliband indicts the Labour Party for failing to accomplish. Through the trades unions and local government, the British working class has produced pragmatic and effective leaders like Bevin or Morrison, who despised ideology and theorizing and were conservative with a small 'c'.

I can imagine many who would say they showed good sense and that what we need now is a Labour *government*, and anything that diminishes our chances of getting one must be shelved. There is no doubt that the Labour Party must and should concentrate its efforts on gaining a parliamentary majority at the next election. Given our political system there is no option; it is the only means of changing central government decision-making. But before we become convinced of the virtue of taking the political landscape as it is and start talking about policies for a hypothetical Labour government, we should first ask *why* we have no option and what this absence of an option does to our politics and our policies.

The Labour administration of 1974–79 had 'policies' – some good, some bad and some indifferent from a radical and socialist point of view. My point is not that Labour failed to carry out its 1973 'Programme'; that kind of constitutionalist cretinism is a symptom of the disease, not a cure for it. Most of the Left would like to 'use' the existing parliamentary system in a way mainstream Labour politicians have allegedly failed to do in order to deliver more radical reforms outside of Westminster. If many of the policies pursued by Labour between 1974 and 1979 are now in tatters or were immediately contradicted by the incoming Conservative administration, it is unlikely much would remain of the 1973 programme had it been implemented. Rather than itching to get back into the 'driving seat', to undo the mess the Tories have made, we should first look at the sort of vehicle a Labour administration will be sitting in – if our hopes come true – in 1988. We should first take a hard look at the British state and political system.

How should we characterize it? Almost everyone will call it a 'democracy', with declining degrees of enthusiasm from Mrs Thatcher to E. P. Thompson. But we all know there is no such thing as 'democracy' pure and simple, even if we restrict the meaning of the concept as narrowly as representative government. On the contrary, we constantly contest the meaning of the word democracy and in doing so accept that there is a wide variety of political mechanisms concealed behind it. 'Democracy' always means a specific combination of political mechanisms: voting systems, types of representative assembly, forms of control of governmental agency, and regulative and constitutional–legal framework. Such combinations have definite political consequences and were often deliberately designed with such consequences in mind or are now endorsed because of the effects they are perceived to have: the constitution of the Fifth Republic was fine-tuned to keep the Gaullists in power; our voting system has been favoured by both Labour and Conservatives because it was perceived to have the effect of working against third parties, etc. Such combinations of political mechanisms are never even-handed; they 'represent' different political forces more or less adequately; they may virtually prohibit others from being formed; they give governments greater or lesser powers; etc. 'Democracy' is an eminently questionable good in the sense that different institutional frameworks favour different social and political forces, *but* the *status quo* is attacked and defended in terms of claims to its being less or more 'democratic'.

It follows that there are many different standards by which we can measure how 'democratic' a political system is. These standards in turn depend on what one expects the political machinery to do. 'Democracy' – as specific combinations of political mechanisms – is always a means or medium to political objectives. Our judgement of the appropriateness of existing means depends on what we expect of politics. Even on the issue of how the people are to be 'represented' there is ample room for disagreement about objectives. One could construct two polar opposites: on the one hand, those who favour responsiveness to popular opinion and seek the accurate reflection of its composition will probably favour frequent elections, radical proportional representation, plebiscites, etc., whilst, on the other, those who see elections merely as a periodically necessary choice between governing elites and who favour stable government will prefer less frequent elections, high percentage quotas for the election of representatives under proportional representation, or a first-past-the-post-system, legal and financial qualifications for political parties, etc.

Most modern debate about the effectiveness of 'democracy' concerns the degree of representativeness of electoral procedures. In the UK, for example, the controversy over proportional represen-tation for parliamentary elections or the challenge by the Tories that the unions are 'undemocratic' both take this form. Such debate centres on who can vote, how often, by what mechanisms, and for what candidates. It takes as the primary objective the *selection* of personnel to form the membership of rule- and decision-making bodies. But it seldom takes the objective further and assesses 'democraticness' by what those representative personnel *do*. That is obvious – they make rules, laws, decisions, etc., according to the constitutional procedures laid down.

The emphasis on representativeness conceals a great flaw in the doctrines of 'representative' democracy, one exposed most ably by, among others, G. D. H. Cole. Representatives do not 'represent' anything; they are elected. Once elected they answer to numerous pressures and constraints, including subsequent re-election, but for them actually to 'represent' the wills of their constituents is impossible. Cole favoured 'functional democracy' as an answer to this problem – a decentralized participatory system of self-management bodies in which no such problem would arise. Curiously, his standard of measure of democracy is still that political mechanisms give effect to the will of the people and he saw guild socialism accomplishing this where the doctrine of the people sovereign through their representatives cannot. Cole substituted giving real effect to the wills of actual people, necessarily complex and diverse, for the fiction of the will of a collective being given effect through a majority of them voting for a person who joins a body that accomplishes certain special tasks. Cole would rather have his actual and diverse people accomplsih their aims, particularly chosen tasks, themselves.

The problem with Cole's vision of pluralistic self-management is that it sets its face against the twentieth century: it ignores the rise of big government and the administration of mass welfare, both of which were making gigantic strides at the very point when Cole elaborated his theory during World War I. But if Cole's vision was obsolete in 1920, what of the nineteenth-century liberal doctrine of representative government and parliamentary sovereignty that he was challenging? It has fitted big government like a glove. Representative government provides legitimacy in deriving the authority of decision-makers formally from the will of the governed, and parliamentary sovereignty clothes the actions of state in a loosely fitting legality that enables and seldom restrains. 'Democratic' politics has given extra tasks to government – mass administration and mass welfare. It has largely ignored one professed goal of nineteenth-century bourgeois liberalism – the construction of constitutional restraints on state authority – or rather it has everywhere left those restraints largely as they were when the object to be restrained was a 'nightwatchman' state and the purpose of restraint was the 'liberty' of the bourgeoisie.

The objective of supervising and controlling major decisions of political and administrative bodies by forces and agencies far wider than a narrow circle of formally responsible decision-makers is historically an important part of 'democracy'. It tends to be stated, if at all today, in the form of 'popular' democracy. Although it is clear that the popular participatory tradition, whether libertarian–populist or Marxist, has been utterly marginalized in Western Europe, we should ask why. First, like Cole's functional democracy, it ignores the rise and success of big government in the twentieth century; but ideas seldom fail to carry conviction simply because they are wrong or obsolete. Second, the popular revolutionary movement, artisan and petty bourgeois in character, was everywhere defeated in Europe by the 1870s and thereafter replaced by the organized workers' movement. When participatory self-administration is expounded it is now a minor part of the Sunday School talk of mass bureaucratic organizations – communist parties. If the objective of containing and rendering accountable big government is to be given effective expression in contemporary politics, it cannot take a populist revolutionary form; it must be one compatible with the constitutional reform of parliamentary democracy.

To return to the UK political scene. 'Representativeness' dominates debates about democracy. Other objectives and other standards of measurement of how 'democratic' our system is are virtually ignored. Indeed, 'representativeness' tends to be marginalized too: it was the losers in the existing electoral system, the Liberals, who wanted proportional representation and in a form that would exclude smaller parties. Moreover, when the question of 'representativeness' is raised it is often used in a way that treats existing parliamentary institutions as the norm against which other practices are measured, as with the Tories' or the SDP's challenges to the unions. If the question of which standards were appropriate to judge our institutions were genuinely raised, it would also open up the issue of the existence of different *doctrines* of democracy and thereby indicate a possible plurality of political objectives and institutional mechanisms, which could only embarrass those who gain most from the *status quo*. Until recently, both major political parties were happy enough to treat our present institutional arrangements as 'democratic' *tout court*. In particular, UK political opinion has taken almost no interest in measuring our institutions against those of other countries.

The main reason for this is that the existing system has suited most members of the 'political class' – those who live off politics and who hold or expect to hold office. Once they are elected to office, the British political system imposes few restraints on ministers: Mrs Thatcher's government is not the first to lie to Parliament, to muzzle and manipulate the press and TV, or to use the secret police to spy on political opponents. Tories and Labour have alike shown contempt for EEC institutions and an unwillingness to learn from our neighbours. Senior Labour politicians at the time of the referendum on the EEC produced absurd arguments about the 'sovereignty of Parliament', just as Mrs Thatcher's ministers do now when they seek to crush and hobble elected local governments. On the quiet, all too many members of the Labour Party have been quite happy with those features of the British political system that bring it closer to an elective despotism than a 'democracy'.

Labour has ruled for eighteen of the forty years between 1945 and 1985, and in that time has had ample occasion to abolish the Official Secrets Act, to change the electoral system, to overhaul the administration of justice, etc., etc. In fact, it has twice had parliamentary majorities as crushingly large as Mrs Thatcher enjoys today, but in both cases, in 1945 and in 1966, it made no use of them to reform the political system. I do not assume they betrayed a population secretly thirsting for socialism and political change. Nothing happened because the system suited Labour parliamentarians and ministers and their inaction went unremarked and uncriticized because trades union leaders and Labour voters were quite indifferent to it.

Whether this indifference will continue is a difficult question to answer. Labour's response to Mrs Thatcher's government's exploitation of our political system's tendencies toward elective despotism has been largely conservative – to seek to 'save' the GLC (a Tory creation designed to end Labour's control of the LCC), to 'defend' trades union rights, to 'retain' the political levy, and to protest at the 'abuse' of the Official Secrets Act in the trial of Clive Ponting, etc. One often feels, hearing this rhetoric, that Britain in 1979 must have been much as Labour might like it to be. The various Labour 'Lefts' have participated in these campaigns but they have also staged others, for example to democratize the Labour Party's own machinery. Far from radically changing the practice of Labour as a parliamentary party, internal democratization was intended to change *personnel*, to get more left MPs selected and elected, and also to 'mandate' the Parliamentary Labour Party to use the existing parliamentary and governmental system to carry out left policies. Herzen remarked of the revolutions of 1848 in *From the Other Shore* (1979) that the radical republicans were the greatest *conservatives* – they sought to add a democratic gloss to a dying world.

To avoid this classic trap of radical conservatism, let us adopt an old device of political criticism and look at our 'democracy' as a visiting Martian might. The first point it will note is our electoral system. The Martian will perhaps ask if its purpose is periodically to propel one bundle of politicians into office rather than another. The Martian will certainly not imagine that the task of the system is to give more or less accurate expression to the electors' preferences for the political parties that contest the election by means of the number of representatives in the assembly. A party receives 43 per cent of the votes cast and yet it is awarded a number of seats sufficient to ensure that its will is imposed in the assembly despite the fact that its policies are bitterly unpopular, even with many of its own members.

The second point our Martian will note is that electoral victory causes the majority party's members in the assembly to occupy the highest policy-making posts in the central government. The Martian may remark that the allocation of these posts to members is in the hands of a small group dominated by the party leader and that this gives immense power through patronage and discipline to that group. The Martian will have also noted that the majority party dominates the assembly and that the part of it that occupies the highest decision-making posts dominates the rest of the party.

The third point our visitor will remark on is that the elected assembly has a twofold task: one part is to pass legislation, a process almost wholly in the hands of the government and to which the assembly gives legality through assent, and the other is to superintend the workings of the government as an administrative machine putting those legislative measures into effect. Perhaps our Martian is a cynic and will note that the former task gravely inhibits the latter. The visitor may also recognize that much of the legislation consists in the permissive extension of administrative power, and that the elected decision-makers are merely the short-term and largely unprofessional heads of a continuously operated administrative machine. He may then find that the policies of this complex of administrative agencies are largely self-initiated and self-regulated, and that the flow of information about them to members of the assembly and the public is closely guarded.

Our visitor turns on the native guides and remarks that things seem as badly ordered here as on its own planet – but that this is not surprising; just as on Mars hardly anyone seems to care. If I have said our system exhibits tendencies toward 'elective despotism' it is because so little detailed supervision or restraint is offered to executive power rather than that executive power seizes an unwarranted and illegal sphere of action. It would be naive to imagine, however, that detailed supervision and control could be exercised primarily from within Parliament over the multiform activities of the machinery of big government. The very model of liberal parliamentarism prohibits this – it supposes law and a legislative assembly as providing the framework within which policy and administration are the execution of previously determined purposes. Things have simply never worked in this way; legislation has permitted the mushroom growth of government agencies. Similarly, to imagine that the formal answerability of ministers to Parliament imposes a serious check on the ramified and multiform structure of big government is little short of absurd.

If we consider a major objective of a 'democratic' political machinery to be the supervision and control of continuously functioning big government, then we should have to admit that by this standard our system is a failure. It cannot be said that the 'on the shelf' proposals for reform would act as more than palliatives:

(1)　the introduction of proportional representation would certainly weaken the tendencies to 'elective despotism' but, in so far as it promoted centrism and coalitions, it would strengthen the

position of the continuing unelected officials and the 'depart-
ment view';
(2) the further strengthening of House of Commons' Select
     Committees would not hurt, but it would still be a matter of
     trying to extract information from a remarkably tight-lipped
     administrative machine;
(3) the same has to be said of a Freedom of Information Act;
     valuable as it might be, it involves seeking what government
     departments wish to hide and even with a reform of the Official
     Secrets Act there are ample pressures to enforce official silence.

These are not arguments against such measures but they point to the
need for something else – the democratization of government *from
within*. Popular and participatory democracy has always failed as a
general doctrine of democracy because it sought to create a world
where there would be no specialist and hierarchical administrations.
Administrative decisions would be confined to those simple enough
to be performed by participatory self-management methods and by
delegate bodies. Lenin, within a short time of writing *The State and
Revolution* (1917), was insisting on the need to utilize 'bourgeois'
specialists; he did not imagine the Red Army or the national railways
could be run like an anarchists' club. As a result of this failure, little
attention has been given to combinations of representative and participatory democracy, specialist administration and self-management. If we want to 'democratize' government we should look in this
direction, toward the combination of representative democracy with
other forms of representation of social and political forces. I want to
suggest that the institutional proposals of the critics of parliamentary
democracy in the first two decades of this century have some merit
if they are not seen as outright replacements for representative
government and specialist administration. I shall refer to three: participation and self-management, corporatism and inspectorates.

   Before doing so, I must return to the question of 'socialism'.
Socialist political ideas have shown a remarkable diversity in the two
hundred or so years of their existence, ranging from centralized
statism and authoritarian planning to libertarian self-management in
a decentralized economy and polity. Socialist practice has shown
much less diversity. Where democratic socialist parties have succeeded in introducing radical reforms, the 'socialization' of sectors of

the economy has taken the form of giving more and more tasks to the state. The successful 'carriers' of socialism have been hierarchically controlled mass organizations – political parties and trades unions. They succeeded because they fitted in well with the dominant political trends: the rise of a mass electorate and the rise of big government. Parties succeeded because they could compete for voters and offer the prospect of altering the policies of government if they won. Trades unions succeeded because both government and corporate capitalists could bargain with them as agencies representing labour that were considered to possess the monopoly power to make those bargains stick.

It would be idle to imagine things could have been very different. Indeed, libertarian socialists like Cole were drawn into the dominant organizations of the labour movement because of the urgent demands of practical politics. Democratic socialism has relied on utilizing the powers of big government to give it leverage on the private sector and as a means of organizing the 'socialized' components of the economy. But socialism can mean little as a *political* doctrine if it does not attempt radically to change patterns of effective possession of, and disposition over, economic resources. Such socialist change must involve changing the balance of decision-making toward the workers rather than management, that is, giving workers some measure of effective disposition over the resources of their enterprises and industries.

By 'workers' I do not merely mean manual workers or industrial workers – even in successful industrial economies the manufacturing sectors' share of employment is shrinking. Nor do I imagine 'management' can be dispensed with – specialist administrative and hierarchical organization is in many cases indispensable. The 'economy' and 'workers' extend far beyond factories and marketed services. The UK between 1945 and 1979 socialized a vast portion of its 'economy', if you apply the simple test of asking whether activities could be run by private capitalists offering them at a price. Public hospitals, schools, old people's homes, sewerage works, and so on, can be regarded as socialized enterprises and the majority of their employees as 'workers'.

Mrs Thatcher has realized this with a clarity that has escaped socialists; we have been too busy saying how these 'socialized' enterprises have failed to meet our goals to see what they represent.

She sees virtually the whole public sector of the economy and the welfare state as an enemy, which indeed it is to her dogmatic vision of private enterprise capitalism. Mrs Thatcher has two answers to such enterprises: to sell them off, or to insist on the power of management to 'manage' within ever-tighter budgetary constraints. It is here that we may have the chance to propose extending democracy and not alienating the electorate. Countering big government from the bottom up, by democratizing its decision-making and management processes, may come to seem attractive to many civil servants, NHS employees, etc.

A democratic socialist society must be 'pluralist'. We are all aware of the consequences of the attempt to centralize all economic decision-making in the state planning apparatus and all political authority in the leadership of one party. But the competition of a number of independent political parties for the vote is by no means a guarantee of effective 'pluralism' in a broader sense. Indeed, the doctrine of the 'sovereignty' of the elected assembly, far from permitting the supervision of big government by parliamentary means, leads to the state being the primary beneficiary of this claim to concentrated and centralized authority. Government is the executor of the 'sovereign will' of Parliament.

'Pluralism' cannot be confined to representative government, but must also mean – in Cole's sense – the diffusion of decision-making authority. Socialists have generally favoured centralization and concentration of governmental authority, the better to deal with big business. Perhaps they should now favour a broader 'pluralism', the better to tackle big government. That must mean, in the long run, forgoing some of the apparent benefits of electoral victory and 'office'. Such a pluralist system would increase the number of autonomous decision-making centres and entail that these centres' decision-making processes include a substantial element of collective responsibility and self-management. Such a pluralism can go a long way to accomplishing the *political* task assigned to markets by Conservatives – to prevent the growth of control by centralized administrative fiat.

How could this be done? First, we should look to the most radical possible introduction of 'industrial democracy'. This should involve the democratization of decision-making in workplaces in both private firms and public sector agencies like nationalized industries and hospitals. It is difficult to legislate for organizational particularity and complexity and, therefore, no particular mechanism should be dismissed in principle – from self-managing worker-owned cooperatives to workers' representatives on boards of management. If we treat public sector agencies as socialized enterprises – hospitals, schools, etc. – then by means of industrial democracy we could begin to devolve hierarchical organization downwards, by giving employees collective responsibility, and also democratize them upwards, for example by filling some of the places on the management boards of health authorities with representatives of self-managing hospital staffs. Proponents of such 'democratization' often counterpose participatory to representative democracy as if 'real' democracy can be located in one set of institutional means; they also suppose that it is appropriate for all purposes. Clearly, at both 'enterprise' and 'industry' level the two forms have to be combined; the higher the level of decision-making, the less scope for directly participatory methods.

Second, participatory democracy, self-management, collective responsibility and representation on higher organs are devices that should be extended not merely to 'enterprises' but to central and local government administration itself. Why it should be widely imagined that such 'democratization' would damage parliamentary democracy is difficult to understand. At present, 'management' in the civil service has great autonomy in practice: many important decisions are made that never come near the detailed scrutiny of a junior minister, let alone Parliament. If administration were democratized – working practices made subject to consultation, inspection and overseeing of departmental activities by elected committees, promotion and reviews democratized, lower-level tasks self-managed, etc. – then the odds are we would have a much more open and accountable government administration. To imagine we could really have 'open government' or a workable Freedom of Information Act without such change is naive. For government to be permeable outwards it must be accountable internally – 'accountable' not merely upwards to superiors but to diverse agencies and levels within.

Self-managing and democratized enterprises and state agencies will not automaticaly make the right decisions and are not guaranteed to behave well. 'Democratization' cannot be an end in itself, for good or ill. On the contrary, we expect of self-managing and

democratized bodies higher standards of efficiency in the performance of their task, accessibility and accountability. We shall not
always find it.

Democratization and decentralization, pluralism and self-
management, pose complex problems of coordination, assessment
of efficiency, maintenance of common standards, and so on. It
would be idle to deny this, to imagine that one can dispense with
higher authority, planning and supervision. But accountability
upwards to superiors is not the only means of accomplishing this.
There are two other methods, which I shall call 'corporatism' and
'inspectorates'.

'Corporatism' has become an entirely negative political concept. It
first earned odium after its introduction in Mussolini's Italy as an
undemocratic substitute for representative democracy. Corporatist
doctrine helped to discredit the previously influential radical critique
of parliamentary democracy, for fascism was in the vanguard of that
critique. It was then used in the 1960s and 1970s by predominantly
leftist critics, like Leo Panich, as a means of denouncing the
incorporation of union leaders into the governmental process as a
means of controlling their members. But if we define 'corporatism'
broadly to mean the institutionalized representation of organized
interests then it has some positive value. Corporatist representation
is an important concomitant of mechanisms of democratization of
enterprises and state agencies. Corporatism is an essential element in
making such democratization work. It provides a means whereby
those interested in an area of activity or service may have a say in how
it is run or performed even if they are not directly involved in
producing or delivering it. Consumer associations are an obvious
example. They might be directly represented on boards of management where this was appropriate; in this way they could both gain
information and influence, whilst having the liberty to withdraw and
campaign about the activity or service externally. Such associations
already represent recipients of health care and education, claimants,
etc., as well as consumers of single-supplier products like the postal
service or the electricity industry. However, they are marginalized in
relation to management in their areas of activity.

One great advantage of a substantial corporatist component in
a wider political system is that it forces us, in devising such
representation, to ask what 'interests' matter, and why – in particular

to consider not only strongly organized interests and lobbies but also those interests that are poorly organized or unorganized. A formal system of corporatism has the advantage that it provides channels of influence for those without the informal power to lobby that stems from prestige or possession of resources. Corporate representation is always of concrete organizations and interests, for example, the CBI, the Claimants' Union, etc. It is not an abstract and universal representation, as is representative democracy where each MP is claimed to 'represent' a certain number of electors in a locality. I would contend that it would be of political advantage to develop more direct corporatist representation in our national political system – for example, replacing the informal corporatism of the House of Lords with a formally corporatist upper chamber. The direct representation of interests is one valuable means of coordination and supervision.

Inspectorates involve another method of supervision and maintenance of common standards that has occupied a marginal place in socialist political theory. In many areas of administration, specialist knowledge is necessary in order to be able to assess competence or efficiency. Inspection played an important role in the social reforms of the nineteenth century, in areas such as factory safety, public health and educational standards. We still rely on these nineteenth-century achievements to the point where we have become blasé about them. It is evident, however, that we have little to be complacent about and that the strengthening of inspectorates and the standards they police is necessary today in areas such as nuclear, chemical and pharmaceutical safety. But the form of inspection I am advocating here is concerned not primarily with such public regulatory activities, but rather with the supervision and overseeing of administrative policy and performance. In a system in which decision-making was extensively decentralized and democratized, the need for such means of ensuring policy and practice did not diverge too far between the different centres would become even more necessary than it is today. Inspection also offers a corrective to the possible dangers to the public of a democratized system. Democratized and self-managing agencies may make decisions that damage consumers' interests or the public interest just as readily as non-accountable managements, and may feel they have greater legitimacy in persisting in them. I do not think this is a Benthamite fantasy; rather it is an inevitable concomitant of extending democracy. Likewise, I do not think that it would be impossible to find competent and disinterested inspectors, as many on the Left who instinctively distrust 'professionals' might. In the absence of such specific mechanisms of supervision and coordination, the task will tend to fall into even less competent and certainly more mendacious hands, those of the English judiciary.

I realize that a programme of wholesale constitutional and administrative change is the last thing Labour needs as part of its manifesto at the next election. But we cannot leave things as they are for ever. We must start criticizing the *status quo* and perhaps introducing pilot schemes to test the feasibility of democratization and self-management in the public sector. In the short run, most administrative and managerial personnel will seek relief from the Tories' high-handed and capricious meddling. In the long run, if we are serious about socialism we must begin to end the reign of 'business as usual' in government.

NOTE

1   Cole has been extensively cited in earlier chapters. The earlier works of Laski such as *Studies in the Problem of Sovereignty* and *Authority in the Modern State* are hard to come by, but his *A Grammar of Politics* (fifth edition) (1967) still contains strong echoes of his earlier position. For the Webbs see their *Constitution for a Socialist Commonwealth of Great Britain* (1920). European socialists at this time took British political theory seriously as Karl Renner's (1921) review of Cole and the Webbs demonstrates.

6 Does Industrial Democracy Have a Future?

One is tempted, looking at the current situation, to make this chapter very short and answer with a simple 'no!'. The EEC is the sole significant force keeping the issue of industrial democracy on the UK political agenda. Both the British government and the CBI have indicated their hostility to the European Commission's draft Fifth Directive on company law, which outlines a minimum Community-wide framework for workers' participation in enterprise decision-making – and also to the Vredeling proposals on the employee's right to know.[1] Evidence suggests that this dusty response from the government and the employers may not be unpopular or even a matter for concern. This is not simply because of hostility to the EEC or because the Fifth Directive's proposals are less than radical. Union leaderships have evinced little active support for and a good deal of hostility to previous proposals for industrial democracy. Union memberships are hardly thirsting for social change. A majority of both the general public and trades union members appear to believe that organized labour, in the shape of the unions, already has 'too much power' and broadly favours the government's legislation on trades union rights.[2]

If official and popular attitudes make depressing reading, it can hardly be said that the economic situation or the organizational position of firms and unions is favourable to industrial democracy. The dramatic rise of unemployment since 1979 has husked a good deal of the traditional manufacturing sector. Mrs Thatcher's government is by no means exclusively to blame – between 1966 and 1982 the manufacturing sector lost some 3 million jobs. Before Mrs Thatcher's rise to power this trend was partly hidden by the parallel increase of some 1½ million marketed-service sector and public sector jobs. Now employment in the public sector too has ceased to grow as a matter of deliberate policy. Marketed services cannot make up the employment shortfall caused by de-industrialization and demographic trends, even if the government were to follow a reflationary policy. Moreover, new jobs in this sector will tend to be low-paid or part-time.

Whoever or whatever is to blame, job losses in engineering, in hitherto prosperous areas like the West Midlands for example, have dealt the skilled and semi-skilled male industrial working class a heavy blow. In consequence, union memberships are falling in major unions in the manufacturing sector, like the AUEW. As in the 1930s, the unions have been thrown into a cautious defensive stance and, as then, they can expect little or nothing from an unsympathetic government determined to follow an economic strategy based on 'sound finance'. If we turn from the regions and industries that have suffered heavy job losses to the limited areas of industrial and semi-industrial growth, such as 'M4 land', East Anglia, etc., then one finds a very different pattern of labour relations: lower levels of unionization and no regional history of active unionism such as one finds in major industrial labour centres. British firms are increasingly multi-industry, multi-plant and multi-locational groups of companies, often with no apparent economic rhyme or reason. Such firms offer intractable diffculties to effective industrial democracy, or even to inter-site union action. Developments of this kind are painful for the unions and the Left to comprehend, let alone swallow. Tony Lane was reviled for pointing to these all-too-obvious facts,[3] but they pose severe difficulties for industrial democracy if one believes its foundations to be an active trade unionism, with a supporting local political culture, and enterprises of a scale such that plant-level workers can play a genuine part in decision-making.

In 1977 – a mere nine years ago – the picture looked very different, if, that is, one was an optimistic supporter of apparently obtainable measures of industrial democracy. Union membership had been steadily rising since 1945, average incomes had more than kept pace with inflation, and unemployment – above 1 million and rising – had not apparently moved beyond the point where it either exceeded the capacities of macroeconomic management to reduce it, or struck seriously at the membership and finances of the unions. The Labour Party was in power, having been put there in large measure because of the unions' resistance to the Heath government. The unions through the TUC were playing an active part in shaping economic policy and, as their reward for striking the Social Compact bargain, had received such valuable extensions of trade union power as the repeal of the 1971 Industrial Relations Act, the Health and Safety at Work Act (1974) and the Employment Protection Act (1975). Indeed, such was the apparent extension of official union power that many social science commentators began to talk about a new 'corporatism', sections of the Left to bemoan the 'statization' of the labour movement, and sections of the Right to fear for the continued sway of market relations and for the 'sovereignty' of Parliament. The Report of the Royal Commission on Industrial Democracy (1977), which appeared under the chairmanship of Lord Bullock, might have appeared in this context to be the culminating element in this extension of the powers of organized labour. It proposed the statutory representation of workers on the boards of directors of companies with more than 2,000 employees, and this representation was to be through a 'single channel', that is, the trades unions in the company. The scheme of representation was to be organized by the unions among themselves.

At least some of the signatories of the Majority Report appear to have conceived it in this way.[4] The Report – and Lord Bullock probably drafted this portion himself – placed its proposals in the context of a 'magnificent journey' of political reform and the extension of democratic rights. Legislation to grant the workers a say in the governance of their firms was intended to be another step towards the completion of the edifice of political, welfare and citizenship rights that would enable the working classes to play a full part in society. This process of progressive enfranchisement was viewed as constructive and as securing the social foundations of a mixed economy. Industrial democracy would help to cure the 'British disease'. By conferring 'a new legitimacy for the exercise of the management function' (Bullock, 1977, p. 28) – in that labour would be democratically represented in the highest council of management decision-making – the twin ills of industrial conflict and restrictive working practices would be avoided in the interests of industrial efficiency and growth.

The magnificent journey stopped there. The Report was rejected by virtually everybody – employers, unions and political parties. No one wanted this proposed keystone in the architecture of the social democratic state. Lord Bullock's historical process dating back to the Reform Act of 1832 had no future. The rejection of Bullock showed that there was no consensus in favour of a moderate and modernizing policy of reform of the institutional structures of industry: unions wished to be left free to bargain, managers free to manage. In fact, British unions were and are ill-equipped to play the part of active participants in the reform of industry. The Bullock Committee's version of industrial democracy never had a chance, despite the intelligence of its architects and the closeness of some of them to the practicalities of the labour movement. Despite the fears of the emergence of a corporate state in which organized labour would be one of the three main pillars, the unions refused to seize or fight for an opportunity to obtain greater influence. If industrial democracy does come about in the UK it will be by a different route and with very different structures from those proposed by Bullock.

Gloomy though the outlook may appear in 1985, there are good reasons to believe that industrial democracy remains a vital, if virtually unarticulated, political issue. This is not because it is just possible that the Labour Party may be able to form a majority government at the next general election, or that sections of its left wing make noises about industrial democracy. The Labour Party has no proposals as intelligent or radical as the Bullock Report. The reason for mild optimism is, paradoxically, the parlous state and dismal prospects of the UK manufacturing sector. Mrs Thatcher's government has neither revitalized UK industrial investment nor led UK firms towards new high-growth technologies. *If* this sector is to be transformed, *if* new investment is to lead to dramatic growth in productivity, *if* the consequent probable further fall in manufacturing employment is to be managed and accepted by the workforces, then very radical changes will have to be made in the way industry is run. The unions in the private sector may be battered, but they are not broken; they still have it in their power to resist technical modernization that takes place entirely at the workers' expense. Even if one's goals were as narrow as increased productive efficiency and profitability, the need for radical changes in management and working practices and, therefore, in authority relations ought to be apparent.

Industrial democracy remains an issue – avoidable and escapable, but at a definite and high cost – because Bullock was right about the *purposes* of industrial democracy; as right as his committee was probably wrong about the manner of achieving it and the method of representation to be used. British industry in the next twenty years will indeed require a 'new legitimacy for the exercise of the mangement function' if the UK is to remain a major manufacturing and exporting country. We need to look for that legitimacy not merely in formal assent given through elected representatives of labour on management boards, but in the active participation of the workforce in other levels of decision-making, in the transformation and simplification of the organizational structures of firms, and in the transformation of the hierarchies that characterize the division of labour in enterprises.

Such a new legitimacy, based on extensive participation and representation of the workforce, should serve to strengthen the management *function*, although not necessarily the existing management personnel and their prerogatives. This needs to be stressed for two reasons. First, many senior managers will accept participation and representation only if it makes the workers docile and leaves their own powers untouched. Hence the need to stress the legitimation of the *function* rather than of the existing management personnel. Second, if senior managers are ill-equipped to adjust to the necessities of industrial democracy, so too are its most ardent advocates – those who argue for the replacement of existing management structures by 'workers' control'. I stress this because it is all too easy to counterpose a nebulous and ambiguous goal of 'workers' control' to any current attempt to extend in some specific way the say employees have in enterprise decision-making. No advocate of workers' control has to my knowledge explained how an enterprise like ICI is to be *effectively* rather than formally worker-managed, and, if it is argued that industrial agglomerations like this are to be broken up, how the component parts are to meet international competition and retain export markets. Some companies certainly could operate with a simpler organizational structure or be broken into smaller component firms; others could not. Improvements in enterprise democracy will be difficult enough to achieve, without being saddled with critics who denigrate them because they are less than 'workers' control'. I take it as axiomatic that even an extensive package of participation and representation for the workforce in medium-to-large enterprises will not remove the need for either specialist managerial personnel, skills and decision-making structures or some measure of accountability to the providers of external capital funds to the enterprise – be those providers central state agencies, local government enterprise boards, employee-managed pension funds, financial institutions, or conventional shareholders.

The UK has no attractive future as the world's first systematically de-industrialized country; certainly not if one wishes to see a more just and equal society with adequate provision for health, education and welfare. In the next twenty years or so, oil production will progressively diminish in its contribution to UK output and we face in consequence a steady worsening of the balance of payments, unless, that is, something dramatic happens to UK manufacturing industry. To cope with this challenge, we need to begin a process of extensive industrial investment, organizational change and social modernization as soon as possible. Even if the manufacturing sector's contribution to employment diminishes, and it will do so to the extent that the goals of technical modernization and productive efficiency are met (to well below 20 per cent of the employed labour force), it will remain *the* crucial component of a developed high income per capita economy. The centrality of the manufacturing sector in terms of economic structure, output and contribution to the balance of payments is not dependent on the proportion of the labour force employed in it. This is the fallacy of most 'post-industrial' thinking and only fools take solace in the notion of Britain as a post-industrial society. It is the performance of the manufacturing sector that ultimately sustains employment in both marketed and public services.

These arguments are fairly widely recognized. The Conservatives have stressed, correctly (one's political opponents are not always wrong), that promoting increased industrial efficiency and competitiveness in manufacturing has little to do with employment creation. The government stresses the need for new industrial investment, the development of new technologies, and greater productivity; however, it is very bad at facilitating the attainment of these objectives. The one area where the argument has yet to sink in, at least publicly, is the Labour Left. The centrepiece of most versions of the 'Alternative Economic Strategy' (AES) is 'industrial regeneration' based on the state-controlled redirection of investment, which is supposed to lead to economic recovery and go some greater or lesser way towards reducing unemployment. The AES might have worked – in the sense of adding to existing capacity and employment by stimulating growth – *if* employment in the manufacturing sector had not been shrinking dramatically before the 1979 government-induced acceleration of the depression, *if* the UK manufacturing sector were stronger in its grip on the home market and more efficient, and *if* demographic trends had not led to an increase in the numbers looking for work. The AES has been premised on building up and extending a supposedly healthy industrial base, neglected by profit-hungry rentier investors, and with it industrial employment. I have reason to doubt this supposition of health, since manufacturing employment has been contracting for some time and the process of penetration of foreign manufactured goods has proceeded side by side with it. One need not favour the policies that have exaggerated this shake-out to perceive how uncompetitive and over-manned a good deal of UK manufacturing industry has been. If the AES had operated over the post-1979 period, it would at best have shored up existing enterprises and existing working practices. 'Job-saving' investment is certainly not to be condemned – it is a humane objective – but by and large it might be said to defer a growing crisis of competitiveness in the UK economy, which is particularly exposed by its need to maintain and to improve its export performance.

The Conservatives at least have the merit, if few others, of realizing that an *efficient* manufacturing/export sector will not contribute directly to reducing unemployment. The AES in most of its formulations envisages industrial democracy of some kind and extensive nationalization. It does so whilst leaving existing union structures and working practices intact, and on the supposition of rising employment in industry. Industrial democracy can be lightly proposed and involves few real costs; workers and unions need to change very little. This probably accounts for the curious sketchiness of most AES proposals for industrial democracy. If, on the contrary, we assume falling employment in manufacturing, working practices changing dramatically with new investment, and union structures and organizations struggling to adapt to changed conditions, then we have to spell out what industrial democracy is for and why it matters to workers.

If we accept that the modernization of the manufacturing/export sector will lead to further job losses, then we must look carefully at the routes by which that end might be attained. The first may be called the 'Management Road'. It is the one favoured by the present government and consists broadly in a defence of management authority and prerogatives against the resistance of workers. It is supposed that if unions can be weakened by every means possible and unemployment is high, then change can be driven through. The new technology can be introduced and consequent job losses cushioned by dividing workers in different plants and sections within plants so that those in work are blackmailed out of supporting their newly redundant colleagues. In more enlightened firms this may be compensated for by pay-offs and paternalism – IBM style – particularly if the firm is a non-union one.

What is wrong with this 'road'? One does not have to have even the remotest sympathy for the rights of organized labour to see the gaping holes in it. First, it supposes a period of systematic depression and mass unemployment to provide the requisite 'discipline' (recovery would tend to undermine such 'discipline', even as it stimulated demand). A prolonged depression of home demand will tend to stimulate only rationalization and job losses to meet a fixed or shrinking market share. Firms will on average tend to adjust output to a stagnant market rather than seek to increase market share. Secondly, it assumes that reduced and rationalized workforces will be loyal, docile and de-unionized. But one can rationalize to the point where there is little room for manoeuvre, and on such a scale of operations unions can mount a counter-offensive, even if they have failed to resist job losses successfully. Thirdly, it neglects the fact that the active cooperation of the workforce is required if new technology is to be fully exploited and if a reduced labour force is to perform as required. It is doubtful if this can be bought and very doubtful that it can be bullied out of workers by fear of the sack. Paradoxically, the 'management road' threatens to restore just the lacklustre productivity performance it seeks to avoid. Micros and robots may mean fewer workers but those workers' active and intelligent contribution to work probably becomes more not less important.

If job losses have to be borne, on pain of a less than radical transformation in our manufacturing performance, the one route likely to succeed is the one that offers the manufacturing labour force the maximum of compensatory advantage. Much of this advantage cannot be provided within the private sector industrial enterprise: any enterprise-based measures must be complemented by alternative job creation by central and local government, a genuine retraining initiative, state subsidy of alternative forms of work participation and civilized standards of support for the unemployed. Without such public policies, workforces will resist further job losses with justified vigour. However, compensatory advantage in the enterprise must be offered too. If workers are not to be locked into resistance to new products, new technologies and new working practices, they must be given a real say in initiating and organizing them. It is to be hoped that, looking at the costs in terms of 'jobs' eliminated or forgone, they will seek strategies that combine efficient working with the maximum number of persons employed. Unions have been singularly ineffective at maintaining the levels of employment of their members and have tended to resist some of the more imaginative ways to increase the aggregate levels of employment. Workers with some say about the future may well be more sympathetic to job-sharing, reducing overtime, earlier retirement or part-retirement, and so on.

A genuine part in decision-making for the workforce means the acquisition of managerial skills by that workforce. The Bullock Report was clear on the massive training effort that would be needed, and its proposals for training and specialist support were among its most radical aspects. To give a new legitimacy to the management function implies that workers both understand and in part *exercise* that function – not all workers (that is utopian in the present context), but an active and committed minority sufficient to inform, guide and lead their colleagues. If this sounds 'elitist', it is no more than the realities of the shop stewards' task today in respect of union affairs. The new information and control technologies need not further subordinate workers to senior management decisions and supervision; indeed, in the right social context they offer the means to decentralize a portion of decision-making and control.

It should not be thought that 'industrial democracy' has a place only in manufacturing industry. If the UK manufacturing sector faces a crisis that demands radical changes in the way it is run and such that the workers are given substantial responsibility for success or failure, a problem of equivalent seriousness but of rather different sources faces a good deal of public sector services. Low economic growth, a continuing large number of unemployed and an ageing population are not problems that can be conjured away, whatever government is in power. A significant increase in the portion of GNP devoted to industrial investment will worsen rather than ease the problem of resources for the public sector services in the short to medium term. Public services will be under severe pressure in terms of both demands for health, education and welfare resources and constraints on their supply. Public sector employment and output are the obvious candidates for 'rationalization' in this context. But surely we want to increase aggregate employment, not reduce it, and unemployment and demographic changes mean that demands for public services will be rising not falling. We need, therefore, to maximize the efficient delivery of services. A more self-managed, less hierarchical set of local and central government services may well be one answer – tiers of officials raised one upon another don't come cheap. Supposing that there are the necessary disciplines of budgetary controls, statutory duties and inspectorates, then self-management could get more public servants performing 'front line' tasks.

It is often objected that 'industrial democracy' in the public sector is inappropriate because it interferes with the 'sovereignty of Parliament', with central government authority, with the rights of the local electorate, and with the powers of senior local authority officers to manage. Why Parliament should be any more 'sovereign' if Fords at Dagenham has some measure of 'industrial democracy', but the local DHSS office does not, defeats me. Parliament is no more 'sovereign' in the web of state bureaucracies, influential private lobbies and big corporations than the Austro-Hungarian Emperor Ferdinand I who was finally driven to say to his domineering servants: 'I am the Emperor and I *shall* have dumplings for dinner.' Mrs Thatcher may bully her civil servants but she cannot substitute herself for them or the mass of detailed decisions they daily make. Clearly the *scope* of self-management needs to be specified, but so it would for an autonomous work group running the paint shop at Dagenham. Certainly the public may need to be protected from its self-managing paid servants as from the other kind; but improved statutory rights of access to information, the more thorough specification of statutory duties for public bodies, tougher inspectorates and independent appeal bodies are surely the answer rather than retaining an official hierarchy that is only answerable upwards.

Like 'corporatism', the threat to parliamentary 'sovereignty' from the democratization of the public sector is a bogus bogeyman. Modern societies cannot be democratized by representative democracy alone. To plead the superior representativeness of MPs or councillors at the expense of the direct representation of important interests or of self-management is a weak argument. Elections provide legislative and governing bodies with personnel, who have sometimes received the votes of only a small fraction of the eligible electorate. What do these personnel 'represent'? Their own interests? The interests of their parties? The lobbies who pay them or to whom they listen? Those constituents whose wishes they happen to know? Representative democracy certainly has a vital part to play – but because it controls the membership of a portion of the political elite by means of a popular secret ballot that is difficult to rig and not because of the interests those personnel happen to 'represent'. G. D. H. Cole's critique of representative democratic doctrine and his defence of functional democracy is one of the best and most original bits of British social theory; it merits serious attention from the thinking Left today (see Cole, 1917, 1921, and Wright, 1979).

A final reason why industrial democracy may be a vital, if unarticulated, issue on the political agenda is the future of wage determination. Mrs Thatcher's government has dealt with inflation by a programme of policy-induced depression – nominating a large number of persons as 'extra' inflation-fighters by making them unemployed. Despite the present government's deflationary policy, the incomes of those in employment have on average more than kept place with inflation throughout its administration. Indeed, wage settlements in the private sector up until spring 1985 were running above the rate of inflation. The government has used its position as the largest employer both to check public expenditure and to fight inflation by imposing an 'incomes policy' on the public sector through cash limits and corresponding pay norms. If a policy of sustained depression is only partially effective in combating inflation because it does not control private sector wage settlements, then one can begin to see the impact of even a modestly reflationary policy and one that did not operate a dishonest and inequitable de facto 'incomes policy' on the public sector. Sustained recovery requires the control of incomes, whether or not this is done by something called an 'incomes policy'. This is not merely a matter of preventing wage inflation 'overheating' the economy, of short-term crisis management of the first stages of recovery. Sustained recovery based on new industrial investment and a modernization of infrastructures implies a dramatic upward shift in the portion of GNP devoted to investment and a decline in the portion devoted to consumption. Reducing overseas investment or redirecting existing savings alone cannot accomplish this task. If it is accepted that we need to invest much more in manufacturing, that service industries will continue to claim their share of investment funds, that housing and infrastructure investment need to be increased, that we wish to halt the run-down levels of public services and cannot finance state expenditure and investment wholly by higher levels of borrowing, then levels of personal income will be under severe constraint and average living standards will in all probability have to *fall* in the short term. It is deeply dishonest to suggest otherwise. Such a fall is not easy to engineer if one is operating a policy of systematic depression and is evidently very difficult if one is attempting to stimulate the economy. A package of wage and price controls, tax measures, and so on, is inevitable if the aims of economic policy are to reflate, to favour the poor and lower paid, and to favour industrial investment. This package will not stop at the threshholds of the wealthy or the middle classes, and if it were to work it would make a great deal of the wage-bargaining powers of trade unions at plant and enterprise level meaningless.

I have argued elsewhere that if the necessities of controlling inflation and of industrial expansion must lead to a significant loss in local collective-bargaining capability then workers must be offered some real compensation and protection in the shape of a greater say in enterprise decision-making and, through the TUC, some clout in national economic affairs (Hirst 1981, 1982). The point to emphasize here is that the weakening of enterprise collective bargaining on wages issues, a more rationalized and centralized policy of wage determination, and a policy of 'wage solidarity' toward the lower paid do not mean that the unions nationally and collectively in the TUC will be weak in consequence. Swedish unions and the LO did not lack political influence under exactly these conditions in the period of uninterrupted post-war Social Democratic rule.

Mrs Thatcher's attack on trades unions and their rights makes the issue of the *radical* reform of the unions a political hot potato. But it can be argued that the unions need to be induced in the direction of organizational and operational change from a left-wing more clearly than from a right-wing point of view. The free marketeers dream of abolishing trades unions, and yet all but the most brain-damaged of them know that modern managerial and corporate capitalism cannot do without them. This reduces the extreme Right to the role of a small dog yapping at the postman's heels: they can annoy and even hurt, but they cannot taste red meat.

To take two examples of the need to re-think left attitudes on union practices, both related to industrial democracy: the closed shop and combine committees. Bullock favoured enterprises with 2,000 employees and over as the cut-off point for its starting proposals, because unionization in such enterprises was at a level of some 80 per cent. Clearly, many of these enterprises operate closed-shop agreements, and this in part explains the high level of unionization. But, as Tony Lane has pointed out, is a high level of automatic official unionization by means of the closed shop better than a lower level of active unionism without it? Evidence suggests that many managements, in contrast to their 'political' spokesmen, have tended to favour closed-shop policies because it gave them certainty about their negotiating partners and the disciplinary capacity of those partners to enforce agreements.[5] Just as many managements have favoured the closed shop, so many unions have been less than sympathetic to inter-union and enterprise inter-site combine committees because they endow the workforce as a whole with organizational capacities and leadership that are not subject to direct control by national occupationally based unions.[6] Industrial democracy would necessarily facilitate the growth of analogues of such committees, perhaps with more extensive powers. Even the Bullock proposals, which stressed the union-based 'single channel', envisaged creating a Joint Representation Committee in each enterprise; this forum was concerned with board-level representation arrangements but could nevertheless serve as a means of stimulating combine committees in those plants and companies that did not already have them.

In my earlier articles on industrial democracy, I defended Bullock's conception of a 'single channel' of representation controlled by the trades unions. I did so for two reasons: first, because the unions could probably undermine and make a mockery of any representative machinery they did not favour, and, second, because a non-union-based representative machinery, even if notional and ineffective, might be used formally to legitimate management policy against the unions. I have rather grudgingly changed my mind about the 'single channel' as circumstances have changed. In 1977 the best role for 'industrial democracy' – workers' representation on management boards – was as an adjunct to and a catalyst for extended collective bargaining. Statutory requirements for representation on company boards would act as a catalyst to drag willing and unwilling unions into a wider role.

The main reasons why I would now reject Bullock's 'single channel' and, indeed, a single scheme of representation to be imposed wholesale and statutorily, are as follows:

(1)   Bullock makes it clear that a high level of unionization is a prerequisite for this method. Only very high levels of unioniz-ation in an enterprise can make the 'single channel' look democratic. The problem here is the cut-off point of 2,000 employees. It is in the smaller (perhaps single-site) firm that workers will find it easiest to participate, to understand its workings and to begin to exercise the management function. If such firms are less unionized, then a 'one person one vote' system and a workers' council are the more effective and just ways to move forward.

(2)   The company board is not necessarily the first or most vital place to introduce 'industrial democracy'. Lower-level experi-ence of self-management in autonomous working groups, participation in production planning, and so on, can provide genuine knowledge and benefits that might build a basis of interest in and preparation for board-level representation. Worker directors stuck on top of a hierarchically managed workforce will accomplish little more than discrediting indus-trial democracy (to be fair to the Majority on the Bullock Committee, they did want more than that). At the same time it must be accepted that the procedures with which one begins must offer some substantial mixture of participation in, and influence over, consequential decision-making. Beginning at a

level where workers *can* be effectively and quickly influential
does not imply a lesser extent of challenge to management
prerogatives. Managers may tolerate the odd group of be-
mused ill-informed workers on the board more readily than
autonomous work groups.

(3) Bullock largely ignores the need in industrial democracy to
represent, to involve and to change the working style of
managers. To treat managers as 'bosses' and thereby ignore
them for the purposes of representation may appear fair
enough: why should they be double-counted? They have
power as managers, why give them representation as
'workers'? But one of the main aims of industrial democracy as a *process*, rather than a fixed scheme, is to change
working practices, to stop managers – whether senior or
middle – being 'boss' in the old sense, of issuing commands
that must be obeyed.

(4) A set of measures that did begin to 'democratize' enterprises, to
change attitudes to them on the part of workers and to change
working practices would lead to resistance by at least some
national union organizations and some larger or smaller
portions of the enterprise workforce loyal to those organizations. There is no way of deciding these issues for or against
in the abstract; sometimes the unions will be right and the
workers 'cutting their own throats'. The general point worth
making is that *if* enterprise workforces have some measure of
separate organization from their national unions – such as work
councils, working group general meetings, and committees –
then at least *they* can formulate and pursue such policy lines,
which may end well or badly. We must get over the idea that
unions must be the main and exclusive source of representation
of workers in enterprises. If industrial democracy did succeed in
a company or plant this would necessarily cease to be true; there
would be organizations and forums related to doing the job that
gave workers another voice. The notion of a 'single channel'
betokens a genuine inability to conceive what real success in
industrial democracy would be like, and in fact virtually
guarantees the blocking of that success by putting the unions in
control. If working practices are to change in British industry,
workers will not only have to fight management, they will

need to oppose their own unions and will need the organizational means to do so.

If industrial democracy is to be promoted among a largely hostile
and indifferent workforce, a single industrial democracy statute with
a single main means of representation is not the real answer. Rather
one should look for a 'package' of overlapping measures. Driving
reluctant workforces wholesale into legal minimum schemes will
not promote enterprise democracy as a meaningful goal. In fact the
best way to begin is to try to build up a number of new 'best practice'
technology enterprises in new and expanding industries, probably
with government support, and take industrial democracy as far as it
will go with a new carefully selected workforce. Such enterprises
could serve as laboratories, models and training grounds. The
Labour government in the period 1974–79 invested its limited
energies and funds in saving failed enterprises such as KME, *Scottish
Daily News*, and Meriden. This should by no means be despised and
Tony Benn as industry minister had to fight hard enough for *this*.
But 'rescue' workers' cooperatives cannot represent the main thrust
of industrial democracy and self-management.

Again, Labour in office in the period 1966–70 used the IRC to
further greater concentration and merger and thus helped to foster
the conglomerate/corporate mess we see in so much of British
industrial organization today. A major component of any serious
concern with industrial democracy must be creating enterprises of an
organizational form and scale such that workers can identify with
them and help to manage them. Bullock's proposals for groups of
companies were defective and self-defeating; by conceding to group
management the Report virtually guaranteed that, had it become
law, this trend to complex group organization would have been
reinforced. Much of this organizational structure is neither technically necessary – plant sizes have not followed the corporate concentration and merger moves – nor very efficient – low worker
understanding of and identification with the controlling organization is often coupled with an indifference to its success. Restructur-
ing for workforce manageability is a more economically rational
general aim than building dinosaur big battalions.

Statutory provision there will have to be, to comply with EEC
requirements. Unless sections of British workers, management and

political parties take the issue seriously little genuine industrial democracy will result. It is all too probably the case that political attitudes on the part of workers and unions will not change. To say that industrial democracy is of necessity on the political agenda, however unarticulated as an issue it may be, is not to suppose that there is any inescapable structural logic moving the political organizations and social forces toward tackling it. The point of saying it is a hidden issue on the agenda is to indicate the price to be paid if it is not taken seriously. The plans of Left and Right for industrial reconstruction will either remain largely hot air or unproductively consume substantial investment funds unless workers are motivated to transform the way industry works. The Left needs to recognize that to change workers' relations to work *also* means changing the role and powers of the trade unions as organizations. The Left may entertain radical goals, but it can be extremely conservative about the social institutions with which it identifies. It would be bizarre if industrial democracy changed workers' relations to work and did not transform the unions. Management can be fought and made to concede powers to workers. If the present forms and powers of union organization are made sacrosanct then the battle cannot begin.

NOTES

1   European Communities Commission Background Report, ISEC/B29/ 83 'Worker Participation in Decision Making'.

2   For a relatively recent example of the large number of sources confirming such attitudes see the Marplan poll published in the *Guardian*, 6 February 1984. One should note an encouraging sign in that the poll of trades union members indicates that 40 per cent think present legislation is 'about right' and 37 per cent think it has gone 'too far' – only 14 per cent think it 'not far enough'. In other words, there is no popular basis – among trades unionists – for further sweeping reductions in trades union rights.

   Robert Taylor's *Workers and the New Depression* (1982) is probably the best guide to current problems and attitudes – he makes clear how little shop-floor interest there is in industrial democracy (pp. 145–6) and also the depth of the productivity problem.

3 See Tony Lane (1982) and the subsequent discussion in Communist Party publications.
4 Jack Jones, Clive Jenkins, David Lea of the TUC, Professor K. W. Wedderburn and Professor G. S. Bain were the members of the Committee most likely to take a strongly pro-union view.
5 Taylor is clear that managements have strong reasons to favour the closed shop; the same conclusion emerges from Brown (1981).
6 Lane (1982) makes this point.

7 *The Concept of Punishment*

'Punishment' has become an increasingly problematic and controversial category in the last forty years or so. Particular punishments such as the death penalty have become symbolic of wider political divisions, as the recent controversy in the United Kingdom demonstrated. The opposing forces have fought their symbolic battles over the utility of hanging as a means to an end. Abolitionists argue that it cannot function as a deterrent. Restorationists argue that it would so function and, moreover, in some cases also argue that certain criminals justly deserve to be executed, whatever the deterrent effect of the penalty. In like manner, prisons have become a focus of controversy, which centres on whether or not they 'work'. A substantial libertarian lobby argues that prisons have 'failed'; they serve no purpose but to degrade inmates and to breed hardened criminals and, therefore, should be abolished. A more cautious and conservative economy-minded lobby calls for shorter sentences and more non-custodial sentences for less serious criminals, reserving prison for the most serious cases. By no means incompatible with the latter view is the stridently expressed current of opinion that demands longer sentences for serious crimes, mandatory sentences and more prisons – prisons here being perceived as the most effective means of checking a supposed slide into lawlessness.

It is only apparently paradoxical that both the forces that criticize particular forms of punishment from a libertarian and reformist stance and the forces that berate the present penal regime from a 'law and order' stance help to create a climate of opinion in which modern means of punishment have 'failed'. This climate in large measure derives from viewing particular means of punishment as means to some definite end – a state of affairs that should prevail among the recipients of such means, such as deterrence or reform.[1] One consequence of this 'climate of failure' – given that the vast majority of citizens intuitively sense that some form of penal sanction is necessary – is to give credence to those justifications of punishment and those views of the purpose of punishment that are least concerned with success or failure. I refer here to justifications in terms of 'just deserts', victim satisfaction and 'social defence'.[2] These justifications of and purposes for punishment are the very ones that anybody concerned to minimize the punitiveness of sanctions and who favours the most thorough legal regulation of punishment should fear. Deterrence and reform have been the goals in terms of which reformers have sought to reduce the severity of punishments. The failure to achieve these goals makes it possible to argue for punishments that appear less likely to fail precisely to the degree they approach the ritualistic ends of vengeance and the raising of the morale of the law-abiding.

It is, therefore, far from paradoxical that those who favour the greatest legal protection for those subject to punishment under the law and the least punitive means to stand for sanctions need to know *why* we punish and what the use of penal sanctions can and cannot accomplish. Libertarians who aim for a utopia in which there are no punitive sanctions and ultra-conservatives satisfied with ritualistic vengeance can dispense with the question. Knowing that penal sanctions are necessary to a legal order and that we can accomplish little by means of them – if, that is, the standard of measure of means is some outcome in terms of the behaviour of those to whom they are applied or the community at large – provides a powerful rationale for seeking to reduce to the minimum the coerciveness and suffering entailed in punishments. Educating people not to expect punishment to 'succeed' ought to be a primary liberal goal.

In this chapter I shall try to provide some of the elements of a knowledge of why we punish and what punishment can and cannot accomplish. I shall argue:

(1) that every regime of punishment has always 'failed' – punishment is always in crisis if it is viewed as a means to some typical outcome in respect of the mass of offenders subject to it;

(2) that the punishments that are commonly available at any given time mainly prevail not because they are chosen as the most efficacious means to an end, but because they are consequences of the prevailing mode of social organization;

(3) that we have probably 'invented' all the possible modes of

punishment; novel means to provide sanction to laws lie in the areas of surveillance and supervision, treatment and behaviour modification, but such means tend to undercut our dominant conception of punishment as a legally specified penalty consequent on a particular criminal act – they tend to lead to the policing of categories of 'dangerous' individuals and they tend to give discretion to agencies other than specifically legal ones;

(4) that where possible we should seek non-punitive means to give sanction to legal norms, but that there is an ultimate and inevitable element of coercion underlying any legal order – that is, legal regulation differentiates itself from other rules for conduct by its claim to be dominant and obligatory. In modern states that claim depends ultimately on the legally justified use of force to sustain it.

I shall discuss sanctions and punishment only in so far as they form part of the regulation of the conduct of social agents within a legal order. Other uses of punishment and practices of punishing are subject to legal sanction and regulation: thus parents and teachers may 'punish' children, but certain actions and consequences constitute unlawful harm. It should be clear that the legal regulation of conduct takes a number of forms and does not consist purely in prohibitive norms; for example, law regulates conduct through specifying the statuses and defining the capacities of social agents. Law is in essence a regulatory activity, and all regulation, however 'creative', involves an element of sanction. The claim entailed in a legal order to be both the dominant and an obligatory mode of patterning conduct means that compliance with legal norms is not a matter of 'ought', as in a moral injunction; rather it has the compelling and overriding force of a 'must'. Sanction follows from this claim to dominance and obligatoriness; it is the element of compulsion that gives whatever substance the claim has. All legal orders have a limited capacity to substantiate their claims and compel through sanctions, but most compliance of social agents is as the result of rationales and inducements other than sanctions.

A sanction may be defined as any legally recognized means whereby an attempt is made to ensure conformity with norms. Sanctions and punishments are not co-extensive. A sanction may be the threat of loss of status and, therefore, of some capacity that stems from legal recognition; loss of corporate personality, withdrawal of a licence, etc., are examples of such sanctions. Punishment must therefore be viewed as one means of sanctioning. As such it supposes not just the attempt to ensure conformity with legal norms but the use of some punitive means to ensure such compliance – 'punitive' meaning the imposition of some loss or suffering on the agent. The idea of a penalty cannot escape some utilitarian calculus, however vague and imprecise, of pleasure and pain. Punishments suppose the recipient is an agent, that is, an entity whose behaviour is the result of some capacity for decision and who will exercise that capacity in the appropriate way given a specific pressure to desist from an action. The idea of a penalty does not necessarily imply any moral connotation. We speak of guilt in certain cases and suppose punishment a justified consequence, but other offences that attract penalties are objective and the penalty is a formal consequence and not a 'just desert' in the sense of being merited by a criminal intention of the agent. For example, traffic fines are penalties: they are aimed at reducing regular illegal parking by imposing a cost that is hopefully unacceptable to the motorist. However, they and other punishments often actually function as a 'tariff', which instead of acting as a means to ensure compliance becomes a fee for tolerated illegality, and thus ceases properly speaking to be a penalty.

The notion of punishment supposes some particular method of punishment used to a certain extent. The reason that persons are sentenced to *a* punishment, even if this be an indeterminate period in prison, rather than to whatever amalgam of means happen to prove effective in their case to ensure a commitment to future conformity with norms, is because all forms of legal order regulate not merely the acts of social agents but also the mode in which attempts are made to control or compensate for such acts. Legal regulation does not end with the determination of guilt or fault, but also extends to the consequences that follow from such judgements. 'Punishments' as means to sanction are claimed to be part of the legal order and not some realm of purely administrative and unregulated means exterior to it. Our prisons often appear to be a private empire outside the law, but they are not *claimed* to be so. Were that the case the legal order's claim to dominance and obligatoriness in all spheres would be forfeit. It is the legal regulation of punishment that sets limits to possible punitive means, that specifies a method and extent. Regulation is a process, and it need not be effective – indeed regulation has built in to it the possibility of evasion and failure.

My analysis of the concepts of sanction and punishment (not as 'ideas' but as working social categories) indicates that particular penal means must to some degree be viewed instrumentally in that they represent the means used to sanction and are part of an attempt to ensure conformity with norms. But the predominantly teleological views of punishment go beyond this minimal instrumentalism in that particular penalties are evaluated in terms of whether or not they lead to certain outcomes or states of affairs, for example, deterrence or providing the preconditions for reform. This teleological view of punishment and the consequent standard of evaluation in terms of whether particular penal means 'work' or not is shared by phil-osophers seeking justifications for the right to punish, by pragmatic penal reformers and by social scientists. The problem here is that these teleological views of punishment as instruments tend to roll up a number of distinct issues:

(1)   Penalties are means to sanction conformity with norms. Some such means are inescapable if we are to have a legal order and the claims it makes, but the degree to which any such set of penalties actually does produce the degree of conformity we observe is virtually incalculable. Many factors other than the use of sanctions or the anticipation by actors of their use induce conformity. This point is widely recognized but it tends to be dismissed when viewing punishments instrumentally because it undercuts arguments against a given penalty in terms of its ineffectiveness or in favour of some new or restored penalty because of its greater effectiveness.

(2)   The question of whether punishments 'work' tends to be evaluated in terms of consequent states of affairs, such as deterrence and crime rates. Less attention is devoted to the question of whether given penalties are actually *penal*; that is, whether they lead to a sufficient measure of loss or suffering to be compelling in attaining the particular end supposed. If this question is raised it is usually in the manner that such penalties would be so compelling if they were properly applied and to an appropriate extent.

Philosophical discussions of punishment tend to be instrumentalist and seek a justification in terms of the states of affairs the application of a punishment is intended to bring about. The great bulk of justificatory argument tends to be conducted in utilitarian terms, with 'just deserts' views forming a definite minority. This has recently changed with the 'new retributionism'. Instrumentalism tends to prevail in that:

(1) Liberal accounts of punishment in general raise the question of individual 'rights'. Punishment is thus considered justified if the act punished involves the commensurate violation of the rights of others and if it is no more than sufficient to prevent such violation and is effective in doing so. 'Excessive' punishments and 'ineffective' punishments should therefore be abandoned.

(2) The notions of 'effectiveness' and 'excess' here suppose that punishment is a means–end relation in which some actual state of affairs is attained. Thus punishment may legitimately be conceived as acting as a deterrent, as a basis for reform, etc. Punishments as a mere 'tariff' on conduct or as vengeance are generally condemned by liberals. Tariff, disassociated from deterrence, implies a 'price' for certain acts and, like vengeance, is regarded as irrational. Tariff as deterrence involves the notion that the law serves as a guide to action, that it prevents actions by setting a minimum sufficient level of unacceptable cost. This is the view advanced in Cesare Beccaria's *Dei delitti e delle pene* (1764). It involves the notion of a rational calculating subject, who faced with certain and definite sanctions will weigh the costs and benefits and desist from certain acts. It is also one definite form of stating the lawfulness of punishment – that it involves a known and certain ratio between crimes and offences and sanctions.

Such a 'liberal' justification of punishment is a clear form of the teleological approach to punishment. In a sense, however, *all* legal punishments are conceived to some degree teleologically. Thus to give an example from a non-liberal or pre-liberal conception of punishment, we may consider the *Ancien Régime* conception of *supplice* outlined by Foucault in *Discipline and Punish* (1977). Here the *end* of punishment was the symbolic affirmation of the power of the Sovereign. Punishment served to affirm the priority of the

Crown by the spectacular destruction of the offender. Its end was symbolic and its means expressive – the measured destruction of the body of the offender. But the symbolic–expressive conception of punishment as a means–ends relation was neither limitless nor arbitrary, contrary to the later claims of Enlightenment critics. Definite acts were specified to be done to a regicide, a parricide, a common murderer, etc.; these and no others were deemed appropriate. The Enlightenment critics regarded these punishments as irrational and arbitrary precisely because they could no longer countenance the end towards which such inhumane and barbarous forms of punishment served as means. Punishment, for the Enlightenment reformer, should govern conduct in a differently purposive way: it should reform or deter the offender, and/or deter others from committing similar offences. The spectacular is rejected because it is considered inefficacious for *those* ends.

The modern regime of punishment is generally recognized to have 'failed' in terms of the two dominant ends that governments, prison officials and penologists have claimed for it – deterrence and reform. Rising crime rates and recidivism are widely cited as evidence for this, and in addition many critics and reformers regard prisoners' conditions as offensive to a civilized society. The result is the crisis of confidence in penal means on the part of those who regard them as instruments to attain certain states of affairs. It has to be accepted, however, in a broader sense that 'punishment' – a particular method used to a certain extent – has a degree of failure built into it. This broader sense is that the application of penal means may fail to be 'punitive'; that is, the persons to whom such means are applied may not suffer pain or loss in the manner prescribed or indeed at all. This may seem odd, but I give some examples below – like the not so apocryphal case of the tramp who commits an offence in the *hope* of being sent to prison. Even those who conceive reform and rehabilitation as the end of a penal sentence must nevertheless suppose its application sufficiently compelling that the convicted person sees such an objective as a reasonable alternative to their previous course of action.

Such ironic lack of success does not, however, exhaust punishments' intrinsic capacity for failure. Punishment, in the sense of a particular method used to a particular extent, *stands for* the general requirement of law that its norms be sanctioned. Sanctioning is represented by the action of certain penal means. We may say that penal means are the 'sign' of sanction – they represent it as specific means of compulsion. In this sense the general requirement of legal norms that they be sanctioned is met by some prescribed and definite means. A legal order cannot therefore adjust its means of sanction precisely to each state of affairs and offender in such a way that they are actually compelling; it must use a set of definite penal means. The result is a greater or lesser rate of failure depending upon how far actual states of affairs and offenders differ from the ones supposed in the means available to be applied.

Punishment may fail to sanction because it takes a definite form relative to offences and involves definite penal means. This relation punishment–offence and these penal means always entail and suppose a 'typical' subject or individual in receipt of punishment and to whom the action of these means is punitive. Punishment often fails to produce a punitive effect because the object of the legally specified means is a 'representative individual', i.e. one to whom the means would be necessarily punitive and who would therefore actually suffer those means as sanction. Particular punishments in their legal form, because they are specified and regulated, must make suppositions about the calculation, motives and feelings that individuals 'typically' have. Such typical subjects are presupposed in the particular penal means, but the actual individuals who commit offences are diverse and may not actually suffer in this postulated way when the means are applied to them. The following are examples of this discrepancy between means and supposed effect, between the 'representative individual' and the actual agent responsible for an offence:

* The imprisonment of the desperately poor and homeless, who may actually *commit* offences to get a bed and some food. Prison regimes, however harsh, suppose minimum standards in any system where detention is more than mere incarceration, i.e. where detention is for reform, and/or where social agents are supposed to have certain minimum rights, involving some regard to health and nutrition. Hence in a society where prison conditions are regulated but individuals' 'private' circumstances are less so, certain individuals such as vagrants may actually live in conditions inferior to those of prison populations.[3]

* Fining both the desperately poor or those in receipt of minimum state benefits and the very rich on a fixed scale related to the offence.
* Even execution may not be effectively 'punitive', not merely in the sense that it fails to deter other offenders but in that certain subjects, like political terrorists or members of resistance movements, may actually *seek* execution as a means of martyrdom and propaganda by act.

In each of the above cases, the offence and the conception of the typical subject define the extent and manner of punishment and not the conditions that would be effectively punitive to the actual individuals who commit offences. To be actually punitive to all given individuals, punishments would have to be adjusted precisely to individuals' circumstances. However, this individuated process of making punishments punitive would actually disrupt the notion of an 'end' as the objective of punishment. This is because a genuinely 'punitive' individuated sanction, which really did make an individual suffer, might have to take a form that did not attain the broader end – neither reforming nor deterring. The punitiveness of punishment is designed to *do* something or to serve as a precondition *for* something else – to humiliate, to predispose to rehabilitation, to deter, etc.; it is never an end in itself. Even 'just deserts' or vengeance theories of punishment suppose that the penal means convey a judgement of value or in some way measure the crime; they can fail too.

Furthermore, the adjustment of punishments to individual circumstances would undercut the rule-governed and procedural nature of legal punishment. Notions of a definite 'tariff', of the rights of a subject in law, and of the certainty of the legal process would no longer apply. Rules and forms would pertain to procedures to determine guilt but not to subsequent dispositions. Hence the certainty of the expectations of subjects under law, the comparability of treatment for analogous offences, etc., would be further undercut. This does not apply merely to 'liberal' expectations about the certainty and calculability of law. It applied equally well where, for example, status governed the means of punishment and nobles regarded it as a right and a mark of rank to be beheaded rather than hanged. Limits related to offences and to the status of offenders are no peculiar mark of post-Enlightenment justice but are necessary in any system of procedure where punishments are seen as themselves law-governed and applied according to rules.

Hence views such as Barbara Wootton's (1959), which seek to individuate corrective dispositions in the interests of social control, threaten to move correction outside of a specifically *legal* sphere. Attempts to make the sanctioning of conduct certain in its application to individuals therefore also undercut the very means–ends relation within law that is already made problematic in the use of definite means of punishment related to offences and the status of offenders. The 'punitive' nature of the means used to sanction is therefore always to a degree 'hypothetical'; it involves an hypothesis about the persons who are the objects of punishment and in doing so supposes a 'typical individual' who is being punished. Hence the conditions of 'punishment' as an attainable state of affairs for all individuals are not given in the means that can be legally used. Punishments cannot be wholly individuated *and* remain part of a 'legal order'.

Punishment is therefore always to a degree inadequate and any given penal means cannot merely be evaluated in terms of a means–ends relation. Thus to point out that hanging does not 'work' because it does not deter and that imprisonment does not 'work' because it does not deter or reform (these failures being evidenced by rising rates of capital crimes or rising rates of recidivism) is not to argue against the use of these punishments *per se*. It is to do so only if we accept that such punishments are to be considered *only* as means to those ends. Indeed, such arguments play into the hands of retributionists. Those who are willing to use punishment as a ritual, as a symbol of resolve, or as a sop to victims or those frightened about law and order need to be challenged by arguments other than that punishments do not 'work', because they are willing to forgo the aim of reform and willing to accept that deterrence effects may be weak. Indeed, if they are told that prevailing penal methods do not punish, that merely reinforces their case for a stronger dose of the same or a search for some new method. There are other arguments against hanging – that the process of determining guilt is too fraught with errors and no restitution can be made to the innocent; that the law should not use violent means to prevent violent acts – which do not fall into the retributionist trap. Likewise there are arguments against imprisonment as a general method of punishment – that it is expensive; that it is so destructive of many individuals' capacities that they become unfitted for any kind of normal social life – which escape the same consequence.

Punishment may be 'hypothetical' in its supposed conditions of application but it always takes a definite social form as certain means applied to social agents. These means do not arise simply because of the agitation of reformers or by a policy process that seeks the rational determination of means to ends. Rather, means of punishment are *artefacts of social organization*, the products of definite institutional, technical and discursive conditions in the same way as other artefacts like technologies or built environments. Artefacts can be explained not by their individual 'purpose' alone but by the ensemble of conditions under which such constructions or forms become possible. First, forms of punishment are related to conditions of social and political organization. Thus imprisonment as a form of punishment in itself rather than detention prior to punishment supposes certain capacities on the part of the state to levy taxes and to administer complex organizations. Fines suppose certain social relations of production, i.e. a fairly high level of generalized commodity production and exchange and the mass monetary circulation coincident upon it. Secondly, the procedural forms in law that specify and limit the forms of punishment have complex conditions of existence. Thus John Langbein (1974, 1977) has shown that the inquisitorial procedure that utilized torture to obtain confessions to prove guilt arose because courts and jurists at that time lacked the autonomy to determine the result of a case by the forms of evidence modern courts now find sufficient. A full confession or a complete proof were necessary because state power and its judges were as yet insufficiently insulated from the pressures of the remaining feudal powers, kin groups and confraternities and the mob. Torture was part judicial procedure and part punishment because substantial partial proofs and evidence were necessary in order that it be applied; the criminal accused was thus already in part presumed 'guilty' in order for torture to be applied. Likewise, *supplice* as a form of punishment under the *Ancien Régime* involved a conception of the Sovereign as a *person* whose majesty and whose peace were threatened directly by crime. Crime was a personal offence to the Sovereign because of the form sovereignty took: public power was embodied in the person of the monarch and the claims of law implicated in the personal attributes and dignity of the monarch. *Lèse majesté* was the ultimate form of offence because the person of the Sovereign was central to the claims of the law to be a dominant and obligatory order of regulation of conduct.

Thus forms of procedure and punishment both have definite conditions of existence outside of any reformer or official's conception of a means–ends relation. Likewise limits set by procedure on punishment can arise from conditions quite different from those in modern liberal assumptions. Beccaria's *Dei delitti e delle pene* (1764) is a key reference point for the liberal myth of rational sentencing replacing arbitrary injustice, of punishments fitted to the gravity of the crime. Beccaria's teleological 'political geometry', with its stress on *results*, i.e. the certainty and calculability of the law in its action, exemplifies the instrumentalist way of viewing punishment. In contradistinction to Beccaria, we can say that *there never can be* certain and calculable punishments and that such certainty and calculability in punishment would undercut precisely the forms of procedural certainty Beccaria wished to introduce for punishment, i.e. law as a guide to action and a calculable tariff–deterrent. Beccaria perceives torture and *supplice* as inherently arbitrary and unlimited, signs of the arbitrary power of the *Ancien Régime*. He mistakes the forms of procedural limitation he proposes with the possibilities of limitation *per se*. The procedural limitations of pre-Enlightenment justice appear absurd to him and non-existent. This is evidenced by the remarks of Beccaria's patron, Pietro Verri, who took the trial of the *untori* in seventeenth-century Milan as a classic example of the arbitrariness inherent in any procedure that worked through torture. However, as the novelist and grandson of Beccaria, Alessandro Manzoni (1964), pointed out, the case Verri chose did not prove his point. The confessions of those accused of smearing the poison on the walls of houses in the city were in fact obtained by violating the procedural limits set down by Renaissance jurisconsults for the use of torture. Leading questions, the use of threats and inducements, etc., were expressly forbidden in the guides for procedure written by jurists (see Ruthven, 1978, pp. 16–17). One might as well say that the Smith Act trials in the US proved the inherent arbitrariness of liberal constitutionalism. On the contrary, both periods of 'clear and present danger' merely prove that any system of procedural limits can be violated or cast aside if legal personnel deem certain political objectives or needs of the social order paramount.

Procedural limitations and legally specified means of punishment are thus not specifically post-Enlightenment and 'liberal' phenomena; they existed in Renaissance and *Ancien Régime* legal systems and they involved just the same problematicity in regarding particular forms of punishment as a means to an end. Thus *supplice*, far from necessarily upholding the majesty of the Sovereign and through him the law, actually often served to produce a disorderly legality in which the weakness of the state was revealed and the Sovereign humiliated. Riots at the scaffold, the defiance and fortitude of the victim could mock the sovereign power. The expressive 'end' of *supplice* could thus be undercut and threatened by the means available to make it manifest. Likewise, a person who withstood procedural torture and failed to confess could neither be fully convicted nor have his property confiscated. Torture could lawfully only be used within definite limits – only so much and by prescribed methods. Anyone who could resist or perish in silence could thus retain honour and the family wealth. Procedural limits when properly applied thus prevented torture being an infallible 'means to truth'.

Punishment, because it is an artefact of social organization, thus cannot be considered purely instrumentally as a means to an end that should cease to operate when it 'fails'. Procedural torture and *supplice* failed in some considerable measure throughout the period of their application. The replacement of the *strappado* and the scaffold came about neither because they came to be perceived to be ineffective at a particular time nor because manners changed in the direction of greater 'humanitarianism'. Writers on the legal status of torture were concerned to specify 'humane' methods and limits to procedure. The notions of humanism and enlightenment have no unequivocal social location or an inherent connection with certain procedural limits.[4] Foucault (1977) is correct to look at the conditions underlying a whole regime of punishment and, in relation to these conditions, to situate the distinctive discourses that sustained it. The new punitive means introduced in the eighteenth century, the penitentiary prison, cannot be evaluated solely through the discourses of the reformers, or by means of the supposed 'ends' of punishment (correction, reform and deterrence) enshrined in their programmes, or by the 'failure' of the resulting institutions to attain those ends. As Foucault shows, Beccaria's critique of *Ancien Régime* judicial procedure and punishments noted their 'failure' and yet did not propose imprisonment as an alternative penal method. Instead he proposed forced labour on public works.

Again, in looking at the new 'ends' set up in the means–ends relation of punishment based upon imprisonment, we cannot take those ends as the discourses of reformers like Jeremy Bentham present them. Bentham is utilizing certain social organizational means rather than 'inventing' them, and the means are certainly not confined in their application to penal policy. The objective of correcting individuals through a regime of detention becomes possible as the result of a series of changes in political and social organization. Prisons are merely one of a series of artefacts of social organization – insane asylums, hospitals, workhouses, reformatories for delinquent youth; as a means of punishment they share institutional features and regimes with forms that do not operate according to the same professed ends. That these transformations cannot be explained by the demands of an emergent capitalism is another and broader question we cannot enter into here. Suffice it to say that the regulation of labour and idleness, of madness and mental health, of sickness and social hygiene, of education and the capacities of youth arose as possibilities and became strategies because the powers and forms of the state, economic relations and national wealth, religion and the patterning of conduct changed in a complex ensemble that is not explained by a single causality or reducible to any social 'level' or the 'interests' of any social class. A change in the means of punishment is a part of this ensemble and is not explicable as the discovery of a new means–ends relation by the reformers. It is precisely such a teleological view that vitiates the explanation in D. J. Rothman's otherwise valuable *Discovery of the Asylum* (1971) and demonstrates the value of the questions Foucault asks in *Discipline and Punish* (1977).

I have stressed that the action of a means of punishment is always 'hypothetical' in its relation to specific individuals, but definite means of punishment are not thereby inconsequential in their actual effects on individuals. Means of punishment, precisely because they suppose a 'representative individual' as their object, involve definite forms of individuation. Individuals are constructed as agents before punishments and in legal procedures; they are interpellated *as* the 'representative individuals' these punishments and procedures suppose. Now whilst this may not actually secure a 'punitive effect', subjects are constructed through a certain relation to punishment and this may have effects on them.

To take an example, the effects of the inquisitorial procedure in trials for heresy. Here the subject is interpellated as not merely answerable for conduct, because outward conformity is not a sufficient defence or requirement; rather the object of inquiry is the subject's beliefs and motivations, which are not taken to be manifest givens or wholly conscious. The confession of heresy is thus conditional on a full review of the subject's beliefs and knowledge, since ignorance of doctrine can lead to heresy. A confessed heretic has a definite status, as one specifically subject to religious 'police' and limitations (on residence, confession, associations, etc). The subject is thus interpellated as responsible not merely for conduct but for its own essence, for every thought and desire. Conduct is not merely outwardly patterned, but should be subject to comprehensive internal review. Confession has the object not merely of policing conformity, but of supervising and transforming individuals. Thus a definite form of enforcing conformity *individuates*. Indeed, heresy trials can lead to a simple man of the people being investigated, and his beliefs, thoughts and motivations taken seriously by doctors of theology. A good example is the miller of a small village in seventeenth-century Italy whose case is examined by Carlo Ginzburg (1980). Because Ginzburg uses the trial to get at popular orally circulated beliefs, he concentrates on the figure of the miller. He therefore lays less stress on the form of examination itself, although he does recognize how remarkable it is that such attention should be paid to the beliefs of a simple uneducated man. The inquisitorial procedure used in cases of hersey could thus individuate in complex and often unintended ways.

Prison regimes were intended to individuate in specific ways by many of the reformers – to discipline and to correct but also to produce a self-governing and industrious individual of orderly habits. The intense debate about the respective merits of the Auburn and Philadelphia 'systems' centred on their capacity to transform the prisoner into an obedient and industrious but also repentant and moral individual conscious of guilt. Prison regimes generally failed to accomplish the reforming and philanthropic goals of some of their projectors. If anything, a prolonged period of imprisonment seems to destroy the socially acquired capacities of most inmates, as Cohen and Taylor (1972) demonstrate well. The personal remodelling offered in claims for regimes based on treatment or 'behaviour modification' should be viewed with some scepticism not merely because they often repeat the very claims and methods of the penitentiary reformers but also because they tend to destroy the very notion that punishment has a limited legally specified manner and extent. Beccaria may have been wrong to suppose that we can construct a rational ratio between crimes and penalties and to identify earlier procedural limitations as mere arbitrariness, but the conversion of punishment into 'correction' is to be feared because it places precious few limits on the powers of the correctors.

If we accept that most of the penal methods are either obsolete – such as corporal and capital punishment, banishment and transportation – or substantially ineffective and used because we have no better ideas of new methods – as is the case with imprisonment and the fine – then we should be wary of 'new' methods of giving sanction to legal norms. Often such methods are presented as 'non-penal', but, just as intended penalties may not 'punish', so supposedly non-penal dispositions may in fact inflict considerable suffering and loss. The reason here is a conflict less between the 'representative' and the actual individual, than between the prospects of such organizations and practices and the shabby substance. Caution is required here – supervision, community service orders and juvenile homes outside the prison service are probably no more ineffective than prisons and fines and can be subjected to procedural limits and inspection. The point is not to paint a rosy picture of an effective and cheap set of non-penal and non-custodial means to control or reform offenders. Painting a rosy future for supervision and 'treatment' and denouncing a new 'gulag' run by psychiatrists, social workers, etc., are parallel faults; both overestimate the effectiveness of the methods praised or damned.

To conclude: the sanctioning of legal norms does require an element of compelling force, but, as we have seen, penal methods are generally anything but effective in this capacity. Legal regulation without an element of compulsion underlying its norms is an improbable utopia. The answer to this contradiction is neither to preach the end of the principal method of punishment underlying the rest – imprisonment – because it does not work, nor to seek to 'toughen' prison regimes and lengthen sentences. We are stuck with some level of imprisonment because we have no other ultimate sanction, but we are not stuck with the present average size of prison population, with the condition of our prisons, or with the dismal efforts to educate, retrain and resettle those offenders we end up having to send there. Knowing the limited value of our penal means we should explore the minimum extent of their use; that extent will be dictated not by the objectives of a rational penology but by what the courts, our political representatives and government officials, and the public are willing to bear. How and how much we punish is a political issue, and should not be dictated by a misplaced concern with the degree to which punishments 'work'.

NOTES

1 In the case of deterrence it is not merely or even the recipient of punishment who is to be deterred; those contemplating crimes may be deterred by the fate of offenders even if, as in the case of the death penalty, these offenders have no opportunity to commit further crimes.

2 Even in these cases, there is ample ground for a judgement of failure, since punishment is not conceived as a merely purposeless ritual. 'Just deserts' theories are particularly problematic in that they fail to establish any rational relation between a crime and a particular method and extent of punishment. For example, why should execution be a more 'deserved' punishment than life imprisonment in the case of murderers. Similarly, victim satisfaction, even when it avoids simple vengeance, has no means of demonstrating that victims will be satisfied by a given punishment; they may deem it too much or too little, or believe that no finite punishment measures the crime. Social defence supposes prolonged neutralization – typically a long prison sentence – and is therefore unlikely as a general rationale for dealing with serious offenders: only transportation and penal colonies, with minimal concern for living conditions and mortality, could offer even the mirage of a cheap solution. Social defence by means of non-penal techniques, such as surveillance and supervision or 'treatment', is another matter. On the issue of the difference between punishment and treatment see below.

3 This failure of penal servitude as a form of punishment has been evident since the days of the eighteenth-century reformers. Conservative critics pointed out that the lot of a large section of the free labouring population

was harsher than any prison regime or system of labour service envisioned by the philanthropists and *philosophes* of the Enlightenment. A conservative friar, Ferdinando Facchinei, made this a central point of his criticism of *the* classic text of the reformers, Cesare Beccaria's *Dei delitti e delle pene* (1764). As Franco Venturi observes:

> Father Facchinei had already realised that hard labour would be meaningful only if it were very different from free labour, and if the condition of the convict was substantially changed in relation to the man who had to work to earn his living. Yet, one had only to look around to realise, he said, that this difference did not exist. The poverty of those who worked was such that their situation was not very different from that which Beccaria proposed should be assigned to those sentenced to hard labour. [Venturi, 1971, p. 106]

4 Ruthven (1978), a writer firmly in the liberal humanistic tradition, is nevertheless clear that Renaissance jurisconsults were concerned to introduce procedural norms and 'humane' methods into juridical torture. For a valuable discussion of torture in early-modern and Enlightenment Europe see also Peters (1985).

Bibliography

Adams, P. and Minson, J. (1979), 'A note on the distinction between sexual division and sexual differences', *M/F*, no. 3.

Beccaria, C. (1764), *Dei delitti e delle pene*. Translated 1769 as *Of Crimes and Punishment*. Republished in Manzoni (1964).

Bendersky, J. W. (1983), *Carl Schmitt: Theorist for the Reich* (Princeton, NJ: Princeton University Press).

Bernstein, E. (1899), *Evolutionary Socialism* (New York: Schocken, 1961).

Boyle, K. and Hadden, T. (1985), *Ireland: a Positive Proposal* (Harmondsworth, Middx: Penguin).

Brown, W. (ed.) (1981), *The Changing Contours of British Industrial Relations* (Oxford: Basil Blackwell).

Bullock, A. (1977), *Report of the Committee of Inquiry on Industrial Democracy*, Cmnd 6706 (London: HMSO).

Campbell, T. (1983), *The Left and Rights* (London: Routledge & Kegan Paul).

Cohen, S. and Taylor, L. (1972), *Psychological Survival* (Harmondsworth, Middx: Penguin).

Cole, G. D. H. (1917), *Self-Government in Industry* (London: Hutchinson Educational, 1972).

Cole, G. D. H. (1920), *Guild Socialism Re-Stated* (London: Gollancz).

Cole, G. D. H. (1921), *The Social Theory* (London: Methuen).

Coleman, J. S. (1974), *Power and the Structure of Society* (New York: W. W. Norton).

Dahl, R. A. (1985), *A Preface to Economic Democracy* (Cambridge: Polity Press).

Donzelot, J. (1980), *The Policing of Families* (London: Hutchinson).

Dworkin, R. (1977), *Taking Rights Seriously* (London: Duckworth).

Edelman, B. (1979), *Ownership of the Image* (London: Routledge & Kegan Paul).

Engels, F. (1895), 'Introduction' to *The Class Struggles in France*. In K. Marx, *Selected Works*, Vol. 2, ed., V. Adoratsky (London: Lawrence & Wishart, 1942).

Erjin, Chen (1984), *China, Crossroads Socialism* (London: Verso).

Figgis, J. N. (1913), *Churches in the Modern State* (London: Longmans).

Fine, B. (1984), *Democracy and the Rule of Law* (London: Pluto Press).

Foucault, M. (1972), *The Archaeology of Knowledge* (London: Tavistock).

Foucault, M. (1973), *The Birth of the Clinic* (London: Tavistock).

Foucault, M. (1975), *I, Pierre Rivière* (New York: Pantheon).

Foucault, M. (1977), *Discipline and Punish* (London: Allen & Unwin).

Ginzburg, C. (1980), *The Cheese and the Worms* (London: Routledge & Kegan Paul).

Goode, P. (ed.) (1983), *Karl Kautsky: Selected Political Writings* (London: Macmillan).

Hart, H. L. A. (1961), *The Concept of Law* (Oxford: Clarendon Press).

Herzen, A. (1979), *From the Other Shore* (Oxford: Oxford University Press).

Hindess, B. (1983), *Parliamentary Democracy and Socialist Politics* (London: Routledge & Kegan Paul).

Hirst, P. Q. (1976), *Social Evolution and Sociological Categories* (London: Allen & Unwin).

Hirst, P. Q. (1979), *On Law and Ideology* (London: Macmillan).

Hirst, P. Q. (1981), 'On struggle in the enterprise', in M. Prior (ed.), *The Popular and the Political* (London: Routledge & Kegan Paul).

Hirst, P. Q. (1982), 'The division of labour, incomes policy and industrial democracy', in A. Giddens and G. MacKenzie (eds), *Social Class and the Division of Labour* (Cambridge: Cambridge University Press).

Hirst, P. Q. (1985), *Marxism and Historical Writing* (London: Routledge & Kegan Paul).

Hunt, A. (1982), 'The politics of law and justice', *Politics and Power*, no. 4 (London: Routledge & Kegan Paul).

Jäggi, M. *et al.* (1977), *Red Bologna* (London: Writers and Readers).

Kant, I. (1795), *Perpetual Peace*. In *On History* (Indianapolis, Ill.: Bobbs Merrill, 1963).

Kautsky, K. (1909), *The Road to Power* (Chicago, Illinois: Samuel A. Bloch).

Kautsky, K. (1918), *The Dictatorship of the Proletariat* (Ann Arbor, Mich.: University of Michigan Press, 1964).

Kelsen, H. (1945), *General Theory of Law and the State* (New York: Russell & Russell).

Kelsen, H. (1967), *The Pure Theory of Law* (Berkeley, Calif.: University of California Press).

Kirchheimer, O. (1961), *Political Justice* (Princeton, NJ: Princeton University Press).

Kirchheimer, O. (1969), *Politics, Law and Social Change* (eds. F. S. Burin and K. L. Shell) (New York: Columbia University Press).

Kitching, G. (1983), *Re-thinking Socialism* (London: Methuen).

Lane, T. (1982), 'The Unions: Caught on the Ebb Tide', *Marxism Today*, September.

Langbein, J. H. (1974), *Prosecuting Crime in the Renaissance* (Cambridge, Mass.: Harvard University Press).

Langbein, J. H. (1977), *Torture and the Law of Proof* (Chicago: Chicago University Press).

Laski, H. J. (1967), *A Grammar of Politics*, 5th edn. (London: George Allen & Unwin).

Lea, D. and Young, J. (1984), *What is to be Done about Law and Order?* (Harmondsworth: Penguin).

Lenin, V. I. (1902), 'What is to be Done?'. In *Collected Works*, Vol. 5 (Moscow: Progress Publishers, 1963).

Lenin, V. I. (1917), 'The State and Revolution'. In *Collected Works*, Vol. 25 (Moscow: Progress Publishers, 1963).

Manzoni, A. (1964), *The Column of Infamy* (Oxford: Oxford University Press).

Marx, K. (1871), *The Civil War in France*. In *Selected Works*, Vol. 2, ed. V. Adoratsky (London: Lawrence and Wishart, 1942).

Miliband, R. (1964), *Parliamentary Socialism* (London: Merlin).

Morrison, H. (1954), *Government and Parliament* (Oxford: Oxford University Press).

O'Hagan, T. (1984), *The End of Law?* (Oxford: Basil Blackwell).

Pashukanis, E. G. (1978), *Law and Marxism* (London: Ink Links).

Paton vs Paton and Trustees of BPAS (1978), Transcript: Lee & Nightingale (Liverpool: Shorthand Writers).

Peters, E. (1985), *Torture* (Oxford: Basil Blackwell).

Polan, A. J. (1984), *Lenin and the End of Politics* (London: Methuen).

Renner, K. (1921), 'Democracy and the council system?'. In T. B. Bottomore and P. Goode (eds), *Austro-Marxism* (Oxford: Oxford University Press, 1978).

Rothman, D. J. (1971), *The Discovery of the Asylum* (Boston, Mass.: Little, Brown).

Rousseau, J.-J. (1762), *The Social Contract*. Ed. G. D. H. Cole (London: Everyman edn., Dent, 1913).

Ruthven, M. (1978), *Torture, the Grand Conspiracy* (London: Weidenfeld & Nicolson).

Schmitt, C. (1976), *The Concept of the Political*. Trans. & ed. G. Schwab (New Brunswick, NJ: Rutgers University Press).

Schwab, G. (1970), *The Challenge of the Exception: an Introduction to the Political Ideas of Carl Schmitt between 1921 and 1936* (Berlin: Duncker & Humblot).

Sharlet, R. (1974), 'Pashukanis and the withering away of the law in the

USSR', in S. Fitzpatrick (ed.), *Cultural Revolution in Russia 1928–31* (Bloomington, Ind.: Indiana University Press).

Steenson, G. P. (1979), *Karl Kautsky 1854–1938: Marxism in the Classical Years* (Pittsburgh, PA: University of Pittsburgh Press).

Taylor, R. (1982), *Workers and the New Depression* (London: Macmillan).

Thompson, E. P. (1975), *Whigs and Hunters* (London: Allen Lane).

Tomlinson, J. (1982), *The Unequal Struggle* (London: Methuen).

Venturi, F. (1971), *Utopia and Reform in the Enlightenment* (Cambridge: Cambridge University Press).

Webb, B. & S. (1920), *Constitution for a Socialist Commonwealth of Great Britain* (Cambridge: LSE/Cambridge University Press, 1975).

Weber, M. (1978), *Economy & Society*, 2 vols (Berkeley, Calif.: University of California Press).

Wright, A. W. (1979), *G. D. H. Cole and Socialist Democracy* (Oxford: Oxford University Press).

Wootton, B. (1959), *Social Science and Social Pathology* (London: Allen & Unwin).

Index

An environmentally friendly book printed and bound in England by www.printondemand-worldwide.com

This book is made entirely of chain-of-custody materials; FSC materials for the cover and PEFC materials for the text pages.

#0395 - 270213 - C0 - 234/156/10 - PB